On every stump and fallen log, and on every fork and bulge of living tree, little elves' gardens of small plants and fungi were growing—dainty sprays of vaccinium, red and orange toadstools, barberry, gaultheria; and the roadside banks were set with myriads of ferns, while mosses grew to such size that I sometimes mistook them for a young growth of some stiff, heathery plant.

—*J. Smeaton Chase at Prairie Creek, 1913,* California Coastal Trails

The
HIKER'S
hip pocket
GUIDE
to the
Humboldt
Coast

by
Bob Lorentzen

BORED FEET PUBLICATIONS
MENDOCINO, CALIFORNIA
1988

© 1988, 1989 by Robert S. Lorentzen
First printing, September 1988
Second printing, June 1989
Printed in the United States of America

Illustrations by Joshua Edelman
Symbols by Jann Patterson-Watters and Taylor Cranney
Maps by Bob Lorentzen and USGS
Design by Judy Detrick and Bob Lorentzen
Edited by Anne Fox
Typesetting by Comp-Type, Inc., Fort Bragg, CA
Published by
  Bored Feet Publications
  Post Office Box 1832
  Mendocino, California 95460
  (707) 964-6629

Library of Congress Cataloging-in-Publication Data
Lorentzen, Bob, 1949-
    The hiker's hip pocket guide to the Humboldt coast.
        / by Bob Lorentzen.
      pp. 192
      Bibliography: p. 188
      Includes index
      ISBN 0-939431-01-7
      1. Hiking—California—Humboldt County (Calif.)—
Guide-books.
2. Hiking—California—Del Norte County (Calif.)—Guide-books.
3. Humboldt County (Calif.)—Description and travel—
Guide-books.
4. Del Norte County (Calif.)—Description and travel—
Guide-books.
I. Title.
GV199.42.C22H865   1988 917.94'11—dc19   88-22293
                                                  CIP

10 9 8 7 6 5 4 3 2

Dedicated to Patricia Priano, my partner in life and best friend, who has provided invaluable support and encouragement from the beginning. Without her this book could not have happened.

As Trish would insist, if I were not already adamant about it, this book is also dedicated to California Ocean Sanctuary, the movement to prevent the degradation and destruction that would result if oil exploration and development were allowed on the Humboldt and Mendocino Coast. Save the coast for future generations, whether of people, fish, birds, whales or other life.

NO OFFSHORE OIL!
OCEAN SANCTUARY NOW!

For more information, write:

OCEAN SANCTUARY COORDINATING COMMITTEE
  P.O. Box 498
  Mendocino, CA 95460

In memoriam,
Eris Rasmussen Harman
Glenn Watters
Sam Watnick
Zia Dancer Zuma

ACKNOWLEDGMENTS

I wish to express my hearty thanks to all who helped create this book. In particular, I thank Anne Fox for her enthusiasm and sensitive editing; Joshua Edelman for his great illustrations; May Edelman for her brainstorming at our dining room table; Jann Patterson-Watters for her marvelous symbols and infectious excitement; Margaret Fox for her early feedback, continued support and copying machine; Judy Detrick for the time at her kitchen table and her superb design.

For their early support, enthusiasm and pithy comments, I thank Humboldt County booksellers, especially Carlos Benemann and Char Evans, and Alan and Barbara Wilkinson of Prairie Creek Redwoods State Park. For resourceful and constructive comments, I thank Douglas Warnock, Anne Smith and John Sacklin of Redwood National Park; Bruce Cann of Bureau of Land Management; Joe Hardcastle and co-workers at Humboldt Redwoods State Park; David Hull and Mark Andre of the City of Arcata; Noelle Liebrenz of Wilderness Press; and many others at Prairie Creek Redwoods, Del Norte Coast Redwoods and Patrick's Point State Park.

Thanks also to my dedicated proofreaders, Judith Becker, Ruth Dobberpuhl, Amanda Avery, Chris Hock, Bill Brown, Carol Goodwin-Blick, Maureen Oliva, Karen Timmer, Caitlin Bean, Marsha Green, Gina Salamone; Linda Pack for creative scheduling; Anthony Miksak of the Gallery Bookshop for his outspoken enthusiasm; Jeffery Garcia for companionship on the trails; Taylor Cranney for her help with the symbols.

Special thanks to Paul Smith, his family and friends for their generosity and caring; and to the readers of my *Mendocino Coast* book who have provided constructive criticism, without which this book might never have been completed.

CONTENTS

INTRODUCTION

Humboldt and Del Norte Counties comprise a vast wild land of forests, rivers and shores in the northwestern corner of California. The area's 165-mile coastline varies greatly from north to south. From Crescent City north, the shore consists of sandy beaches backed by marine terraces. South of Crescent City, the rugged rocky shore lies below high, eroded cliffs that stretch to the Humboldt County line. Humboldt County's coast north of Trinidad is characterized by dark sand beaches with high bluffs, rocky coves and tide pools, three large lagoons and vast forests. Then the coast turns more gentle, with long, dune-backed beaches adjacent to fertile river floodplains and the lowlands of Humboldt Bay. South of Ferndale, high coastal mountains drop steeply to the narrow, secluded beaches of California's Lost Coast.

Highway 101 crosses the heart of this rugged land from north to south, providing access to hundreds of miles of trails. Although the highway stays within 25 miles of the shore, roads to the coast are few, except in the vicinity of Humboldt Bay.

This book tells you how to find and walk, hike or ride over 400 miles of trails through this wild, scenic land. The trails range from easy walks to difficult backpacks, with choices to fit the taste of every nature lover. The hikes will lead you to the highest peak on the California Coast, the world's tallest trees, the broad mouths of wild rivers, marshes and estuaries rich in bird life, pristine ponds and streams, city parks, vast wild beaches, meadows and prairies sprinkled with wildflowers, and jagged rock outcrops.

So get out of your car and use feet, bicycle, horse or wheelchair to explore the Humboldt/Del Norte Coast.

HOW TO USE THIS BOOK

The trails in this book are organized from the north to the south. Highway 101 is the starting point for the directions to every trailhead. No trail is more than two hours from Eureka or Arcata.

You will find a milepost number on Highway 101 in the directions to each trail. These numbers refer to the white highway mileposts placed frequently (but at irregular intervals) along Highway 101 by CalTrans, the State Department of Transportation. You can quickly determine the location of a trail (and where it is in relation to you) by referring to its milepost number. The detailed directions to each trailhead may include other mileposts on secondary roads.

You do not have to start at the beginning of the book. Simply turn to the trail nearest your location and you will be on your way. Neighboring trails will be on adjacent pages.

For each trail in the book you will find a map (top is always north), specific directions to the trailhead, the best time to go, appropriate warnings, and a detailed trail description with some history and/or natural history.

You will find a group of symbols below the access information for each trail. They tell you at a glance the level of difficulty, type of trail, whether there is a fee, and whether dogs are allowed. The list of symbols follows.

At the end of the book are appendices that list the trails most suitable for a particular type of recreation: mountain bikes, equestrians, backpacking and handicapped access. Another appendix details the California Coastal Trail as it currently runs through Del Norte and Humboldt Counties.

THE DANGERS
TEN COASTAL COMMANDMENTS

When on the trail, *always* keep your senses wide open. Don't let nature lull you into total complacency. In this way you can best appreciate nature's pleasures, as well as her dangers. Here are ten rules to keep you out of danger, so that you may safely enjoy the beauty of the coast.

1. DON'T LITTER. Most of these places are unspoiled. Do your part to keep them that way. Always hike with a trash bag and use it, even for matches, cigarette butts and bottle caps. I always pick up any trash I see in a pristine spot, my way of saying thanks to Mother Nature.

2. NO TRESPASSING. Property owners have a right to privacy. Stay off private property. There are enough public places without walking through someone's yard.

3. NEVER TURN YOUR BACK ON THE OCEAN. Oversized rogue waves can strike the coast at anytime. They are especially common in winter. They have killed people; watch for them. More subtle are the changes of the tides: don't let rising tides strand you against steep cliffs or on a submerged tidal island. The ocean is icy and unforgiving, generally unsafe for swimming without a wetsuit.

4. STAY BACK FROM CLIFFS. Coastal soils are often unstable. You wouldn't want to fall 40 feet into the icy sea, would you? Don't get too close to the cliff's edge, and never climb on cliffs unless there is a safe trail.

5. WILD THINGS: ANIMAL. All the animal pests of the Humboldt Coast are small, unless you get chased by a Roosevelt elk (generally they will not chase you unless you

THE SYMBOLS

WALK:
Less than 2 miles
Easy terrain

EASY HIKE:
2 to 10 miles
Easy terrain

MODERATE HIKE:
2 to 10 miles
Rougher terrain

DIFFICULT HIKE:
Strenuous terrain
Backpacking possible

MOUNTAIN BIKE
TRAIL

PICNIC SPOT
May be tables or just
a good blanket spot

BIKE TRAIL

DOGS ALLOWED
ON LEASH

CAR CAMPING

WALK-IN OR
BIKE-IN CAMPING:
Environmental camps

TIDEPOOL ACCESS

HANDICAP ACCESS

RECOMMENDED
FOR FAMILIES

INTERPRETIVE
NATURE TRAIL

TRAIL FOR
EQUESTRIANS

RESTROOMS
AVAILABLE

WATER AVAILABLE

FEE AREA

FISHING ACCESS

NO OIL EXPLORATION
OR DRILLING

get too close). Watch out for ticks, wasps, mosquitoes, biting spiders, scorpions and rattlesnakes. Human animals are easily the most dangerous, especially in deer hunting season (from the first week in August until the end of September). Always listen for gunfire, especially outside state parks. *Never* (even in a vehicle) enter an area where logging is in progress. UNDERWATER ANIMALS: When tide pooling or at the beach, always watch for sea urchins and jellyfish. Both have stinging spines that are painful. Remember that mussels are quarantined each year from May through October; at that time they contain deadly poison.

6. WILD THINGS: PLANT. These mean business too, especially poison oak and stinging nettles, which can get you with the slightest touch. Many other plants are poisonous. It is best to not touch any plants unless you know by positive identification that they are safe; this is most important with mushrooms.

7. POT GARDENS. Don't even think about messing with one, no matter whose side you are on. If you ever stumble onto a pot patch, leave more quietly than you came. Take only memories.

8. TRAFFIC. Coast roads are difficult and often overcrowded. Drive carefully and courteously. Please turn out for faster traffic. You will enjoy the coast more if you do. If you stop, pull safely off the road.

9. CRIME. Be sure to lock your car when you leave it at the trailhead. Leave valuables out of sight, or better yet, back at your lodging.

10. ALWAYS TAKE RESPONSIBILITY FOR YOURSELF AND YOUR PARTY. This is a trail guide, not a nursery school. The author cannot and will not be responsible for you in the wilds. Information contained in this book is correct to the best of the author's knowledge. Author and publisher assume no liability for damages arising from errors or omissions. **You must take the responsibility for your safety and health while on these trails.** The coast is still a wild place. Trails may change over time and safety conditions may vary with seasons and tides. Be cautious, heed the above warnings, and always check on local conditions. It is always better to hike with a friend. Know where you can get help in case of emergency.

THE HISTORY

Native Americans have lived along the Humboldt Coast for at least 1000 years, perhaps as long as 5000 years. The cultures of the Tolowa, Yurok, Chilula, Wiyot, Mattole and Sinkyone prospered with the coast's abundant natural resources.

Spanish galleons sailed along the coast beginning in the sixteenth century. The first recorded European visitors came in 1775 when Spanish explorers sailed into Trinidad Bay, met the local Yuroks, and erected a cross on Trinidad Head. Their mapping of Trinidad as a safe harbor brought later explorers. In 1806 an American named Jonathan Winship discovered Humboldt Bay as his ship explored the coast for the Russian-American Fur Company. His discovery was forgotten because he deemed the bay unnavigable for large ships.

In the 1820s and 1830s, fur trappers and explorers made the first overland journeys through Humboldt County. Jedediah Smith, Stephen Meek, Ewing Young, Peter Ogden and three others named McLeod, Mofras and LaFrambois stayed briefly without recording much information about the area.

In July 1848, gold was discovered first on the Trinity River, then on the Klamath. The difficult inland route to these mines provoked the search for safe harbors along the North Coast.

On November 5, 1849, a party of eight explorers left the Trinity mines seeking the Trinidad Bay shown on Spanish maps. They were led by Dr. Josiah Gregg, writer and frontiersman, who made the first extensive record of a visit to Humboldt County. The Indians told Gregg it was an eight-day journey to the coast, so the party set out with enough food for a ten-day journey. Lacking guides, they lost the Indian trail in a snowstorm and struggled through rugged country. The snow turned to rain. By the seventh day they were reduced to eating the flour paste that formed inside their packs. On their journey, they had to cut their way through immense quantities of fallen timber in the vast forests, often progressing only two miles a day. They traveled four and a half weeks to reach the coast.

The starving party arrived at Trinidad Bay on December 7. They traded with the Indians for provisions, then headed south. Crossing the Mad River in Indian canoes, they named it for an argument they had there. They found Humboldt Bay the next evening, and by Christmas Day they camped at the future location of Arcata, feasting on elk and clams provided by the friendly Wiyots.

They headed south to tell California of their discoveries. They named the Eel River as they met Indians fishing for eels (actually lampreys). They named the Van Duzen River for one of their members. Then the eight men separated into two groups. Gregg's group sought a route along the coast, but the rugged country forced them to turn inland south of Cape Mendocino. Gregg died of starvation near Clear Lake. The other group, led by L. K. Wood, followed the Eel River south, faring little better. Wood was mauled by grizzly bears and crippled for life. But they reached Sonoma to report their discoveries on February 17, 1850.

Several ships immediately left San Francisco searching for Humboldt and Trinidad Bays. Settlement began at Trinidad in March, at Humboldt Bay in April. By that summer a trail was completed to the Klamath and Trinity mines. In September the first sawmill opened at Eureka. By 1853 nine mills along Humboldt Bay shipped 20 million board feet of lumber to San Francisco. By 1856 5000 mules were used in the packing business to the northern mines.

The towns of Eureka, Arcata and Trinidad grew and prospered, but not without hostilities from the Indians and natural hardships caused by the wild, rugged country. Eureka became the county seat in May 1856. Humboldt County remained accessible primarily by ship until 1911, when an all-weather road was established to San Francisco.

THE CLIMATE

The climate of the Humboldt Coast is cool, but mild enough for you to hike year-round, if you are prepared for varying conditions. In planning your excursions, keep in mind the following about the seasons along the Humboldt Coast:

November to March are the rainy months, time to bring rain coats and rubber boots. Still, there are often fine sunny days between storms.

April and May are often windy, with occasional rainstorms. The wind may be gentle, or fierce and unrelenting. The landscape is at its most lush and beautiful. Bring layered clothing and hats.

June, July and August bring sunny summer days, alternating with thick fog. You may be comfortable in shorts, but bring layered clothing in case the fog comes in. Sometimes you can beat the fog by heading a few miles inland. (This is the most crowded season, especially August.)

September and October are a beautiful time. Fog is less common. Though there may be rainstorms, most of the days are calm and warm. The land is dry, the hills golden, and the sunsets often spectacular.

15

GET READY, GET SET, HIKE!

You should be chomping at the bit to get out on the trail by now. Here are a few suggestions about what you might need on your hike: layered clothing—sweater, sweatshirt, hat, windbreaker or rain coat; insect repellent; suntan lotion; sunglasses; and small first-aid kit (at least bring moleskin for blisters). Not essential, but highly recommended for all but the shortest walks: water container, extra food, pocket knife, flashlight and extra batteries, matches and fire starter, map, compass (helps if you know how to use it), and of course you would not want to be caught without your *Hiker's hip pocket Guide!*

Additional suggestions: camera; dry socks; binoculars; and field guide to birds, wildflowers and/or trees. If you are backpacking, you should consult an equipment list for that purpose.

When you are on the trail, remember to slow down, open your senses and enjoy. Most people hike at a rate of 2 to 3 miles per hour. But beach sand or steep terrain may slow all but the most hardy to as little as one mile per hour. Leave ample time to do the hike you plan at a pleasant pace. Hike not to count the miles, but for the enjoyment and appreciation of nature. Happy trails to you!

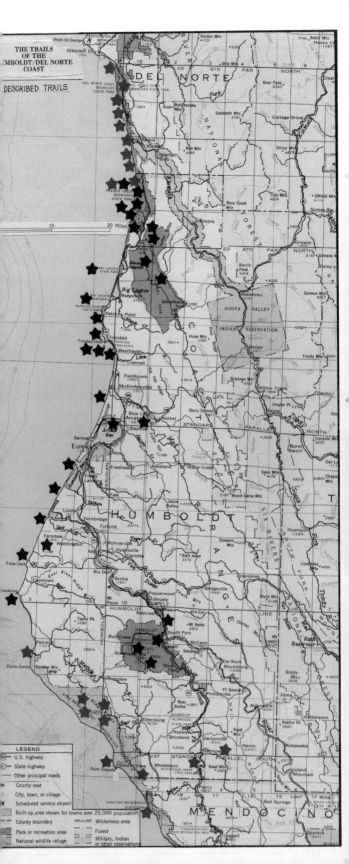

THE TRAILS OF THE HUMBOLDT/DEL NORTE COAST

DESCRIBED TRAILS

LEGEND

U.S. highway
State highway
Other principal roads
County seat
City, town, or village
Scheduled service airport
Built-up area shown for towns over 25,000 population
County boundary
Park or recreation area
National wildlife refuge

Wilderness area
Forest
Military, Indian or other reservations

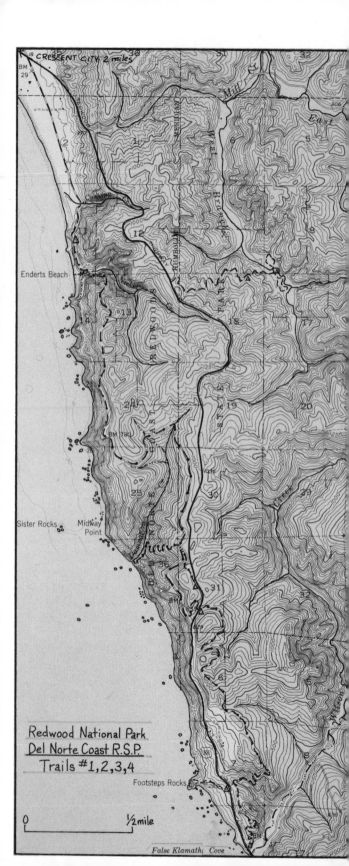

CRESCENT CITY 2 miles

Enderts Beach

Sister Rocks   Midway
                      Point

Redwood National Park
Del Norte Coast R.S.P.
Trails #1,2,3,4

0   ½ mile

Footsteps Rocks

False Klamath Cove

REDWOOD NATIONAL PARK

Redwood National Park comprises 106,000 acres of virgin forests, rugged coastal cliffs and beaches, meadows and streams. In its boundaries are three separately administered state parks—Jedediah Smith, Del Norte Coast and Prairie Creek. Redwood National Park stretches for almost 50 miles from Crescent City in the north to Orick in the south. It includes the traditional territories of three Native American groups who have lived here for centuries: the Tolowa, Yurok and Chilula.

The virgin forests of the park are among the greatest on earth. The redwoods endure from ancient times; as a species they have survived dinosaurs, the Ice Age, and the creation of mountain ranges. Today they stand in awesome silence, catching clouds and fog on their sweeping branches and filtering sunlight with stunning effect. Be forewarned: a walk among these ancient beings will have you craving more.

Redwood National Park was created in 1968 after 50 years of effort. In 1917 the founders of Save-the-Redwoods League toured the groves along newly opened Highway 101 and began to lobby Congress for a park. In 1920 the House of Representatives passed a bill to create a Redwood National Park. But when the bill was defeated in the Senate, efforts turned to creating California state parks. In 1964 a National Geographic article rekindled national park efforts after a survey team from the magazine found the world's tallest tree on private timber land on Redwood Creek. The protracted struggle between logging companies and conservationists ended with the creation of a park of 58,000 acres, the largest national park ever created from privately held lands.

The Tall Tree was saved, but logging continued upstream. Resulting erosion threatened the trees in the new parklands. Another bitter battle led to the expansion of Redwood National Park by 48,000 acres in 1978. Since most of those lands had been clearcut, extensive rehabilitation began in the drainage of Redwood Creek. Over 200 miles of roads and 2000 miles of tractor trails are being removed, the natural contours of the land reshaped, extensive acreage replanted.

The young trail system of the park, already with several fine trails, will be greatly expanded before the year 2000.

1

ENDERTS BEACH
LAST CHANCE SECTION
COASTAL TRAIL
WALK OLD HIGHWAY ABOVE RUGGED COAST

Enderts Beach Road leaves the west side of Highway 101 about two miles south of Crescent City. Today the quiet side road dead-ends at the Enderts Beach Trailhead after just 2.5 miles. But this narrow, winding road was once busy Highway 101, the main artery connecting Del Norte County to the rest of California. Enderts Beach Road and most of the Last Chance Section of the Coastal Trail was the main highway until 1935. It was drivable as a scenic route until about 1970. Part of the old road south of Nickel Creek is on the National Register of Historic Places.

Enderts Beach Road parallels the broad curve of Crescent Beach, which extends for 7 miles south of Crescent City Harbor. It then climbs to Crescent Beach Overlook, a parking area with picnic tables and a view of the rugged coast. Just beyond the Overlook you come to the end of the road and to the start of the Enderts Beach/Last Chance Trail.

The trail may be used for a short day hike to Enderts Beach (one mile round trip), an easy overnight to Nickel Creek Camp (⅞ mile round trip) or the longer, strenuous hike along the Last Chance Section of the Coastal Trail. (For more about the Coastal Trail, see page 180.)

From the trailhead you head south on the old coast highway, descending gradually. You have magnificent views north along Crescent Beach and beyond to Crescent City and Point St. George. You soon pass an old quarry in the cliff to your left. At ⅛ mile you come to an excellent view south to Enderts Beach.

Rock slides cover portions of the road as you descend south. Just beyond ¼ mile from the trailhead, a side trail on the right descends to Enderts Beach. The surf-scoured, sandy pocket beach is small but pretty. At low tide you can explore tide pools here. In summer Park Service naturalists conduct guided walks.

The main coastal trail descends southeast on the old road. Dense vegetation grows here where coastal scrub and forest mingle: Douglas fir, Sitka spruce and red alder mix with silk tassel, coyote brush and berry vines. The trees have been sculptured by the prevailing winds.

Just before ⅜ mile, you bend left and descend into Nickel Creek Canyon. Before you cross the creek, the side trail to the campground heads west to five campsites. You must purify water from the stream.

Then your trail leaves the old highway, turning left and climbing southeast above the creek. At ½ mile your climb steepens. This most strenuous portion of the trail climbs 900 feet in the next 1¼ miles. You turn away from the creek at ⅝

ENDERTS BEACH/LAST CHANCE SECTION
COASTAL TRAIL:

DISTANCE: 1 mile round trip to beach, 7 miles one way on Coastal Trail.

TIME: One hour for beach; 3-4 hours, whole trail (one way).

TERRAIN: Follow old highway along steep coast. Then climb steep hill into virgin forest at headwaters of Damnation Creek.

ELEVATION GAIN/LOSS: To beach: 160 feet+/160 feet-
Coastal Trail, one way: 1400 feet+/680 feet-

BEST TIME: Spring, early summer for wildflowers. When it is not foggy for views.

WARNINGS: Watch for ticks, especially in spring. Trail beyond Nickel Creek is extremely steep. Parking not allowed at southern trailhead (OK at Damnation Creek).

DIRECTIONS TO TRAILHEAD: NORTH END: Turn west off Highway 101 at M.23.03 (Del Norte) onto Enderts Beach Road. Drive 2.5 miles to end of road where trail begins.

SOUTH END: At M.15.6 (Del Norte) on Highway 101 (no parking allowed; park at Damnation Creek Trailhead and walk south).

FURTHER INFO: Redwood National Park (707) 464-6101.

OTHER SUGGESTION: CRESCENT BEACH extends for 7 miles from just south of Crescent City to just north of Crescent Beach Overlook.

THE COASTAL TRAIL runs north of Crescent City, where there are miles of open beach walking to the Oregon border.

JEDEDIAH SMITH REDWOODS STATE PARK lies inland from Crescent City along Highway 199 and the Smith River. Of the several miles of trails, HIOUCHI TRAIL, LITTLE BALD HILLS TRAIL and NICKERSON RANCH TRAIL are particularly recommended. (707) 464-9533.

---

mile, encountering the steepest climb at ¾ mile. About ⅞ mile from the trailhead, you come to a flat spot at a big west bend. This good picnic spot has views down to Enderts Beach. Then head east, climbing more gradually to the one-mile point.

You turn south as your climb steepens briefly, then becomes gradual again. You are now on a ridge with steep drops on both sides. About 1¼ miles you rejoin the old highway and continue to climb south. Wild ginger, with large, fragrant, heart-shaped leaves, grows along the trail.

You reach the first summit at 1½ miles. A healthy young-growth redwood forest grows in an area logged years ago. Descend briefly before a mostly level stretch brings you to a second top at 1⅞ miles. The surf roars from below. Before the second top, you may get a glimpse of the rugged coast.

You begin a steady descent south, dropping 400 feet in the next mile. After a gate, the trail enters an old-growth redwood forest and Del Norte Coast Redwoods State Park at 2⅛ miles. When you meet the power line at 2½ miles, your trail levels briefly, then begins a gradual climb. The terrain drops precipitously to the breakers and offshore rocks below. A fragment of the old highway pavement survives here.

Before 2¾ miles you pass under the power line, with a view of the surf below. You turn east at a spot where the old roadbed survives intact. Your easy climb quickly brings you under the power line again.

At 2⅞ miles an old brass plaque marks Anson Grove. The redwoods grow large as you approach the headwaters of Damnation Creek. Your trail heads south, then bends to the east, climbing gradually. After 3⅛ miles redwood, fir and Sitka spruce grow to 10 feet in diameter along the trail.

You quickly come to a sloughing of the roadbed. Here the powerful geologic forces that shape this coast have toyed with the old road. Then your trail bends left, entering primeval forest. Your trail is mostly level as you curve left, then right, to cross a tributary of Damnation Creek. Rhododendrons thrive in the moist habitat.

Descend gradually to another tributary before 3⅞ miles. You level, then descend to the crossing of Damnation Creek at 4¼ miles. The road has been washed out here. You must cross the creek on a slippery log covered with ferns and redwood sorrel. Be careful!

Climb briefly as you head south away from the creek. At 4½ miles your trail becomes mostly level. You pass several old highway markers. After 4⅞ miles you pass a 14-foot-diameter redwood on your right. Notice the leather fern growing on its south side. You can hear the roar of traffic on Highway 101 less than ¼ mile away. After 5 miles you wind

somewhat but stay generally level, heading south.

At 5⅞ miles you meet the unmarked Damnation Creek Trail. It heads west-southwest from a big bend in the old road, descending 1½ miles to the mouth of the creek (see Trail #2). The trail to the highway is 50 feet beyond, climbing east-southeast. Our trail continues on the old road, descending moderately southeast through a virgin forest of massive trees. At 6 miles you can glimpse the ocean through the trees.

Head southwest now to a big bend at 6¼ miles. The roar of the surf and the barking of sea lions rise from the isolated coast below. You turn southeast and continue level. This easy section of trail winds somewhat. Between 6¾ and 6⅞ miles, the forest below the road thins, providing views of the steep, wild coastline.

At 7 miles a sign points uphill away from the old road. Take this narrow footpath over a small ridge, descending to the highway 7⅛ miles from the trailhead, at M.15.6 on Highway 101. If you continue south on the Coastal Trail, be careful crossing the busy road. A "CT" sign across the highway marks the DeMartin Section of the Coastal Trail.

2.

DAMNATION CREEK

ANCIENT TRAIL TO A HIDDEN COAST

The well-beaten trail climbs northwest into a dense forest of large redwoods and Douglas firs. You climb gradually for ¼ mile, through a lush understory of salal, redwood sorrel, sword and deer ferns, evergreen and red huckleberries, rhododendrons and wild ginger.

After ¼ mile your trail levels, then begins a winding descent. At ½ mile, as you descend steeply by three switchbacks, you can see the ocean through the forest. Descend gradually again, paralleling the old highway below to the west. After a short uphill stretch ⅝ mile from your trailhead, you descend to cross the old road, which is now the Last Chance Section of the Coastal Trail (see Trail #1).

The Damnation Creek Trail follows the roadbed north for 50 feet before turning west-southwest on a gradual descent. The junction is not marked. The trail winds among large, fire-scarred redwoods, heading generally west. At ¾ mile you level briefly. Douglas firs to 8 feet in diameter mix with the giant redwoods here.

You then begin a steady but well-graded descent with frequent switchbacks. The sound of the crashing surf rises from below. At ⅞ mile the deep, rugged canyon of Damnation Creek is visible to the northwest. You continue to descend by switchbacks into the canyon.

Beyond one mile, as the trail switches sharply right, you get your best glimpse yet of the ocean below. Gooseberry and five-finger fern thrive in this moist habitat, along with other redwood understory plants. You descend steeply to 1¼ miles, then level briefly before more switchbacks.

At 1½ miles Sitka spruce begin to dominate the forest, though there are still occasional large redwoods. A spruce on the left is 8 feet in diameter. Standing beside it, you can look down to the mouth of Damnation Creek Canyon, your destination.

After a short level stretch, you descend by two switchbacks followed by steep steps. You continue to descend by more switchbacks. Step carefully over the slippery spruce roots in the trail. You come to a stretch of trail disrupted by a small landslide, where piggyback plants grow profusely. Watch your footing in this spot.

After three more switchbacks, your trail turns south-southwest, paralleling the creek. You are 1¾ miles from the trailhead. Salmon- and thimbleberries grow in a dense thicket between you and the rushing creek. Red alders are

24

DAMNATION CREEK:

DISTANCE: 4¼ miles round trip.

TIME: 2 hours minimum.

TERRAIN: Steep descent to beach at mouth of creek. Steep return.

ELEVATION GAIN/LOSS: 1100 feet+/1100 feet-

BEST TIME: Low tide, spring, late afternoon.

WARNINGS: Steep trail. Take it easy. Do not get trapped on the beach by rising tides.

DIRECTIONS TO TRAILHEAD: On Highway 101, a wide turnout is at M.16.0 (Del Norte), on west side of road. Unmarked trail leaves from upper end of turnout.

FURTHER INFO: Del Norte Coast Redwoods State Park (707) 464-9533.

OTHER SUGGESTION: Del Norte Coast Redwoods State Park has other trails around Mill Creek Campground. Turn east off Highway 101 at M.20.25 (Del Norte). HOBBS WALL TRAIL and MEMORIAL GROVE TRAIL can be reached just after you turn off the highway. ALDER BASIN and MILL CREEK TRAILS start near the entrance to Mill Creek Campground.

the dominant tree in this moist habitat. You can hear the breakers crashing on the rocky beach below.

Your descent steepens at 1⅞ miles. Then your trail bends left and climbs into a side canyon, crossing a small creek. More big spruce roots disrupt the trailbed. You descend gradually, passing through a thicket of alders, willows and berry vines.

At 2 miles enter a second side canyon, crossing its creek on a bridge below twisted Sitka spruce. Pass under a power line as the forest gives way to dense coastal scrub. As the trail levels, you can see the breakers ahead. The trail then forks. If you continue straight, you cross over a small natural arch onto a narrow promontory above the beach. To descend to the mouth of Damnation Creek and the beach, take the right fork before the arch and descend steeply.

If you get here at a high tide of +5.0 feet or more, the beach is almost completely submerged. Do not venture onto the beach at such a high tide. If you are trapped by the rising tide on this rugged, isolated coast, there is no escape! If the tide is low enough (+2.0 feet or less) and ebbing, you can walk

200 feet north along the rocky beach and about ⅛ mile south. During a minus tide you can reach rocky tide pools near the mouth of the creek. In fact the Tolowa Indians used an earlier version of the Damnation Creek Trail to come here to harvest shellfish and seaweed at low tide. The Yuroks may have visited as well.

You can find shelter from the harsh wind in the mouth of the rocky creek canyon. Amidst a pile of huge logs jammed into the creek is the rusted piece of an old ship, remnant of one of the many shipwrecks along this wild coast.

From the bluff above the mouth of the creek, you can look northwest to Sister Rocks. To the south are other rocks, including onshore Footsteps Rocks (247 feet; see Trail #4) and offshore False Klamath Rock (209 feet). Gazing at the razor-edged cliffs along the coast, you might marvel that a trail leads to this special place.

Remember to leave adequate time to climb the 2⅛ miles back to the trailhead (an elevation gain of 1100 feet). Fortunately, the trail is well graded. The steepest portions lie in the first mile from the beach.

3.

DEMARTIN SECTION
COASTAL TRAIL
FORESTS AND GLADES WITH COASTAL VIEWS

The trail heads east from Highway 101 at M.15.6, where a sign reads "CT." You descend by steps and switchbacks to a bridge over a tributary of Wilson Creek at ⅛ mile. Then climb away from the highway, zigzagging east. You pass redwoods and Sitka spruce up to 12 feet in diameter. The trail turns south, climbing through the lush, fern-filled forest by switchbacks. By ¼ mile your climb becomes more gradual, winding through the virgin forest.

At ½ mile you come to a series of rough steps. Your climb continues until you top a small rise at ¾ mile. Your trail turns right and heads south, leveling below a ridge on your right, with a steep canyon on the left. You wind around a gulch at one mile. The trail passes through a walk-through redwood and winds southwest to meet a power line at 1¼ miles. You have a spectacular view down to the rocky coast nearly 1000 feet below. Climb briefly away from the coast. Then at 1⅜ miles, come to another saddle with a coastal view.

You again turn away from the coast and return to the forest. You are soon climbing again, gradually at first, then

DISTANCE: 5 miles one way.

TIME: 2-3 hours one way, 5-6 hours round trip.

TERRAIN: Climb through mixed forest, then descend through coastal prairie with sweeping views. Finally descend into deep Wilson Creek Canyon.

ELEVATION GAIN/LOSS: North-South: 420 feet+/1300 ft-

BEST TIME: Spring for wildflowers.

WARNINGS: Watch for poison oak. No fires at DeMartin Camp.

DIRECTIONS TO TRAILHEAD: NORTH END: On Highway 101 at M.15.6 (Del Norte). Look for signpost marked CT. You must park at M.16.0 and walk south along the highway.

SOUTH END: Just beyond M.12.8 (Del Norte) on Highway 101, at north end of DeMartin Bridge at Wilson Creek, east side of highway.

FURTHER INFO: Del Norte Redwoods State Park (707) 464-9533.

steeply before 1½ miles. You pass a "CT" sign, confirming that you are still on the Coastal Trail. The trail descends after that, as the pounding of surf and barking of sea lions rise from far below.

At 1⅝ miles you climb to rejoin the power line, which you now follow, climbing generally south. Around 1¾ miles the climb becomes very steep before reaching the peak marked 1118 feet on the topo map.

You continue along the power line, making a steep descent to 2 miles. You leave the forest for coastal prairie scattered with alders and dense berry thickets. This glade provides views of the spectacular coast, including False Klamath Cove and False Klamath Rock. The trail follows the power line, descending steeply to 2¼ miles, with views all the way. Then you come to level ground.

In 300 feet a spur trail on the left leads to DeMartin Primitive Campground. The camp on the eastern edge of the DeMartin Prairie has ten sites with tables, bear boxes, a composting toilet and tapped drinking water. No open fires are permitted.

The main trail now heads southeast through alder forest and coastal prairie, bringing you to a pumphouse with a water spigot at 2½ miles. You once again follow the power line. The trail may be confusing in this stretch, where a fire break crosses it. Follow the rough track along the power line past two bends to 2⅝ miles. Then head southeast for a few hundred feet to a junction, where another path on your left leads north to DeMartin Camp. You turn south, descending gradually through grasslands.

Just beyond 2¾ miles, you pass a water tank on the left, surrounded by spruce and alder. Descend gradually to 2⅞ miles, where you come dramatically upon the edge of steep Wilson Creek Canyon. Though the canyon has been logged, the view is spectacular. The trail bends right and descends by many switchbacks. A private residence lies below the trail at 3⅛ miles.

After 3¼ miles your trail heads southwest for ¼ mile on uneven tread. The trail then switches right and goes uphill to gain the top of a narrow ridge, not far from the highway. You follow this ridge, which has broad views of the ocean through the trees, climbing briefly around 3¾ miles.

Your trail switches left and descends steeply to a magnificent view of Footsteps Rocks on the coast to the northwest. Then two more switchbacks bring you back to the edge of Wilson Creek Canyon at 3⅞ miles.

You climb by more short switchbacks to a level stretch at 4 miles. You pass a big rock outcrop on your left, then make a steady descent southeast to 4⅛ miles. You continue to descend by more switchbacks to 4¼ miles. Here your trail turns south-southeast for a relatively straight stretch through more coastal prairie with scattered alders.

This brings you to a confusing unmarked junction. You meet an old road here. You might think that the trail continues south, but instead you make a sharp right turn and follow the road northwest for just 150 feet. There you meet a footpath on your right which you follow through a dense thicket of coastal scrub, continuing southwest.

At 4⅜ miles you switch left and head southeast, paralleling the power line. Continue your descent through open country, with views of False Klamath and Wilson Rocks offshore. Just before 4½ miles, cross under the power line and wind through a berry thicket. Descend a series of long switchbacks through the prairie, then into the forest at 4¾ miles.

Your winding trail descends, crossing seven small boardwalks. The trail levels at 5⅛ miles, coming to an overgrown stretch of old highway and a trail junction. Here you have a decision. In summer you can take the footpath on the far side of the old road. This leads to a bridgeless crossing of Wilson Creek in ⅛ mile, below the highway bridge. But in winter you must turn right and follow the old highway uphill for 300 feet to meet Highway 101 at M.12.8. Then, if you are going to the hostel across the creek or continuing on the Coastal Trail, use extreme caution as you cross the narrow highway bridge. The hostel is located in the beautiful, old two-story house south of the creek and east of the highway.

If you are following the Coastal Trail south from here, the next section follows the beach of False Klamath Cove. Since the beach erodes substantially in winter, it may be passable only at low tide. Detour on the highway shoulder, if necessary. By summer the sands are usually replenished. It is ⅝ mile along the beach from Wilson Creek to the mouth of Lagoon Creek, where you meet the Hidden Beach Section of the Coastal Trail (see Trail #5).

4.

FOOTSTEPS ROCKS
TOWERING ROCKS AT THE SEA'S EDGE

The Footsteps Rocks Trail is easily overlooked in the rush of traffic on Highway 101 at Childs Hill. Yet this short trail provides easy access to views of this rugged and isolated coast at a spectacular spot.

Your trail heads west from the tiny sign marking the trailhead. You descend gradually through a tangle of berry thickets and coastal scrub with scattered alders. At ⅛ mile your trail levels briefly, then descends again, passing alders of 3 feet in diameter.

After a short steep section, the tops of Footsteps Rocks appear ahead. At ¼ mile you angle northwest, continuing your descent. You cross a small bridge and continue to descend as more of the towering rocks come into view. At ⅜

29

DISTANCE: 1 mile round trip.

TIME: 30-60 minutes.

TERRAIN: Gentle descent across coastal prairie to base of impressive rock outcrop.

ELEVATION GAIN/LOSS: 280 feet-/280 feet+ round trip

BEST TIME: Spring for wildflowers, great at sunset.

DIRECTIONS TO TRAILHEAD: On west side of Highway 101, first turnout north of Wilson Creek at M.13.44.

FURTHER INFO: Del Norte Coast Redwoods State Park (707) 464-9533.

mile your trail levels, then climbs briefly. On your right is another rock outcrop; a garden of succulents hangs from the top of its sheer face. The terrain is open and grassy here, with more room for wildflowers. Poppies, lupines and blue flag irises dominate.

Your trail levels and turns west, heading straight for the base of the massive outcrops of dark Franciscan stone. In another 200 feet you are directly below towering rocks rising to 247 feet above sea level. The official trail ends here, but two rough foot trails continue. The left fork descends to meet the rocky shore to the south, accessible only at low tide. The right fork winds around to the immense pile of boulders on the north side of the rocks. A few Sitka spruce struggle to grow in this harsh environment.

The right fork continues another 200 feet before ending atop a pile of jagged dark boulders that seem to have dropped from the imposing cliff above. The north face of Footsteps Rocks rises vertically from this spot. Succulents and coastal scrub dangle precariously from the overhang at the top. Gulls soar on the fierce wind currents around the rocks.

You could sit for hours in this wild place and forget you are only ½ mile from a major highway. Immense breakers roll in from the open ocean and smash against the base of these rocks. The incredibly turbulent waters warn you from approaching too close to shore. One large wave could easily sweep away anyone standing on the lower rocks. Stay back!

Spectacular, rewarding views lie at the trail's end. To the north razor ridges plunge to the sea. The deep canyon of Damnation Creek is the only breach in the vertical coastline. Sisters Rocks cluster offshore. To the south you can see False Klamath Cove, with False Klamath Rock offshore.

South of there the coastline near Hidden Beach hides the mouth of the Klamath River. The high ridges above Big Lagoon rise far to the south. Patrick's Point extends west from there.

If you are here at sunset, be sure to leave 20 minutes of daylight to return to the trailhead.

5.

YUROK LOOP
HIDDEN BEACH COASTAL TRAIL
ENCHANTED COAST NORTH OF KLAMATH

The Yurok tribe of the Klamath River country has always been one of the largest tribes of Native Americans in Northern California. Their territory stretched from Wilson Creek on the north to Little River (south of Trinidad) on the south, and up the Klamath River to Weitchpec.

The Yuroks controlled a land abundant with food along the shore and in the sea and river. This abundance helped them to achieve a complex civilization. They built sturdy houses of split redwood. They carved canoes from whole redwood logs: short, agile boats to navigate the rivers; larger vessels with sails for the powerful ocean. The ocean-going canoes were up to 40 feet long and 5 to 10 feet wide. The Yurok leaders accumulated property—land, slaves and other wealth. They used a 13-month calendar based on the moon and had a monetary system based on dentalium shells. The Yuroks traded with the Tolowas for these shells, which originated far to the north around Puget Sound.

Evidence of Yurok civilization has been traced back 1000 years along this coast. They greeted the Spanish galleons that landed at Trinidad in 1775. When fur trapper and mountain man Jedediah Smith explored this country in 1828, his party camped at Wilson Creek and probably received food and other help from the Yuroks. But when hordes of white men arrived in the 1850s, inevitable conflicts occurred, and the Yuroks were displaced. Still, a large number of Yuroks survived by retreating into the heart of their rugged country. In spite of the conflicts, the Yurok tribe retained a viable culture and is currently growing in number. The south end of this hike ends at Klamath Overlook, which is within the boundary of Yurok land.

The Yurok Loop Trail is a one-mile interpretive trail introducing you to the Yurok culture as it follows an ancient Yurok path along the sea's edge. This short, easy loop connects with the Hidden Beach Section of the Coastal Trail.

31

DISTANCE: 1-mile loop/4 miles one way.

TIME: 30 minutes/2-3 hours.

TERRAIN: Easy loop along lagoon to the shore. Easy hike to Hidden Beach, then climb and descend through forest along rugged coast, coming to steep, grassy headlands overlooking mouth of Klamath River.

ELEVATION GAIN/LOSS: Yurok Loop: 150 feet+/150 feet-
Coastal Trail, North to South: 980 feet+/320 feet-.

BEST TIME: Spring, early summer for wildflowers.

WARNINGS: Poison oak along trail. Watch for ticks, especially in spring.

DIRECTIONS TO TRAILHEAD: NORTH END: Park at the Lagoon Creek Parking Area at M.11.8 (Del Norte) on the west side of Highway 101.

SOUTH END: Turn west off Highway 101 at M.8.2 onto Requa Road. Go 2.5 miles to Klamath Overlook. Trailhead is on south end of parking area.

FURTHER INFO: Redwood National Park (707) 464-6101.

You can follow the Coastal Trail south for 4 miles to overlook the mouth of the Klamath River, the lifeblood of Yurok civilization. (The Coastal Trail also leads north for almost 13 miles. See Trails #1 and 3.)

The trail heads northwest from the north end of the parking area, following the shore of the freshwater pond on Lagoon Creek. This pond was enlarged in 1940 as a log pond for a sawmill. Today the pond is stocked with rainbow trout; its surface provides a home for yellow pond lilies and native and migrating birds. Your trail passes through a thicket of alders and willows, then forks. The right fork leads to Wilson Creek Beach and the Coastal Trail north (see Trail #3). Take the left fork and cross a bridge over Lagoon Creek. Get a brochure for the Yurok Loop at the dispenser west of the bridge.

The trail heads west, climbing a moderate hill into the forest. Then you drop quickly to a clearing overlooking the ocean and the mouth of Lagoon Creek. The original Yurok trail south along the bluffs was improved by the U.S. Army in the 1850s. Pioneer settler Peter Louis DeMartin upgraded the trail to a wagon road in 1889.

The trail follows the shore. Coastal grasslands alternate with coastal scrub of salal, ferns, berry vines and ceanothus. At ¼ mile you come to item #4 in the brochure and a grassy clearing. Offshore a jagged rock pinnacle rises 100 feet from the ocean. The Yuroks referred to it as "the place where bald eagle rests." With luck you might see a bald eagle somewhere along this hike. Farther offshore is the 209-foot-tall sea stack called False Klamath Rock. To the Yuroks it was *olrgr,* meaning "digging place." Yuroks went there to harvest edible brodiaea bulbs.

A short hill brings you to #6 at ⅜ mile. You then enter a forest of alder and spruce, climbing another hill to a rest bench and #7. The Yuroks considered their trails to be living things that could become resentful if travelers did not treat them with respect. An Indian hiker would ask, "May I come this way again?" Along each major trail the Yuroks designated pleasant spots as special resting places. For travelers to pass such spots without taking off their load to rest showed disrespect for the trail.

The trail descends gently, paralleling the shore. False Klamath Rock dwarfs the many other rocks offshore. At ½ mile, the trail forks. To complete the Yurok Loop, go left up a short hill, then descend to the Lagoon Creek pond. As you approach the shore, look for river otters, mountain beavers, herons, egrets and ducks that forage here. The trail crosses the pond and returns to the parking area.

You take the right fork to get to Hidden Beach or continue south along the Coastal Trail. The trail descends slightly, then levels in dense forest. At ⅝ mile you climb gradually. You leave the forest for a spectacular view of Hidden Beach and the rocky coast. Make an easy descent across grasslands at the edge of the forest, leveling at ¾ mile.

You continue along the level, open bluff. After ⅞ mile, the trail re-enters the forest. At one mile you meet the side trail to Hidden Beach. It makes a short descent to the jewel of a beach, tucked in the crook of the rocky point to the south.

The Coastal Trail continues southeast into dense, dark forest. After a milepost indicates 3 miles to the end of the trail, start a steep climb around the high, rocky promontory to the south. Climb steeply to 1¼ miles, then more gradually. At 1⅜ miles you are adjacent to the 223-foot-high point on your right. Continue your climb through the forest, with spectacular views of False Klamath Cove and the rocky coast. Salmon- and huckleberries provide a dense undercover.

After passing a rock outcrop on the left, you climb again. The sound of the surf rises from a cove hiding 200 feet below. At 1¾ miles you descend to cross a small creek, then climb again. The trail veers east into a wooded gulch, then turns back toward the coast at 2 miles.

You make a short descent. Then your trail levels, contouring along the steep hillside. At 2¼ miles you climb again, then make a gradual descent only to climb a steep series of steps, reaching the top at 2⅜ miles.

Your trail levels once again in a lush patch of false lily of the valley. Only the chattering of birds and the distant roar of surf break the silence of the forest. At 2½ miles you descend briefly, then climb for ⅛ mile. You wind through the Sitka spruce forest before descending at 2¾ miles.

You climb steeply through several twists in the trail from 2⅞ miles, to be quickly rewarded as you come to a marvelous view. On a clear day you can see Patrick's Point, 30 miles to the south. The mouth of the Klamath is hidden, but the rest of the rugged coast lies before you. You may hear sea lions barking to the west, 400 feet below.

Most of the rest of the hike traverses the steep grasslands. Your trail descends, then levels, passing blue flag irises. A milepost indicates one mile to go. You veer away from the shore, climbing to 3⅜ miles. As the trail levels, you come to a fence marking the boundary of the Redwood National Park maintenance center. An old softball diamond is east of the fence. The ocean roars from below.

You quickly come to an overlook with a guard rail and rest bench. An interpretive sign explains that the coast here is sinking gradually into the Pacific, unlike most of the coast to the south, which is still rising from the ocean. You can see the broad mouth of the Klamath River.

Your last stretch of trail contours the steep grasslands above the mouth of the Klamath, a prime spot for spring and

summer wildflowers. At 3⅝ miles you pass through a stand of spruce and cross a small creek on a boardwalk. You turn southeast toward the Klamath Overlook Parking Area.

At 3⅞ miles a bench by the trail provides a view of the outlet of the Klamath and the three large sea stacks guarding its mouth. The largest of these is called Oregos after the Yurok spirit who lives there. Yurok legend says that Oregos told the fish when to enter the river and what route to follow upstream.

In another 250 feet, a spur trail on the right winds down to Klamath Overlook in about ½ mile, right above the rock Oregos (no ocean access). The main trail climbs to its end at the parking area. The Coastal Trail continues on the south side of the Klamath, but you need a car to get there, unless you can convince a fisherman with a boat to ferry you across the river. It is 7 miles by road, about 3 miles by the river to Flint Ridge Trailhead.

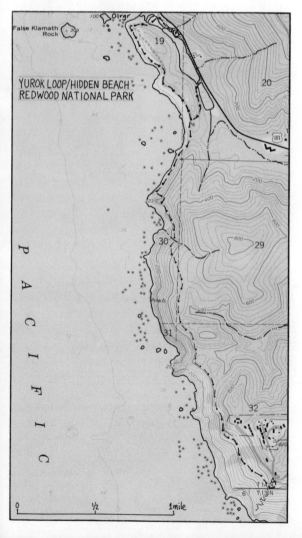

YUROK LOOP/HIDDEN BEACH
REDWOOD NATIONAL PARK

DISTANCE: 4½ miles one way, 9 miles round trip.

TIME: 2½ hours each way.

TERRAIN: Along a lakeshore, then climb to a coastal ridge of virgin redwoods, following it to descend near the ocean.

ELEVATION GAIN/LOSS: 880 feet+/460 feet-, east to west. 1340 feet+/-, round trip

BEST TIME: Spring for wildflowers. Any clear day.

DIRECTIONS TO TRAILHEAD: EAST END: Turn west off Highway 101 at M.3.75 (Del Norte) onto Klamath Beach Road. Go 1.5 miles to Alder Camp Road junction, where there is a parking area. Trailhead is just downhill.

WEST END: See Coastal Drive.

FURTHER INFO: Redwood National Park (707) 464-6101.

6.

FLINT RIDGE SECTION
COASTAL TRAIL

VIRGIN FOREST ABOVE THE KLAMATH

The mighty Klamath River empties into the Pacific just 3 miles downstream from the Douglas Bridge parking area, the eastern trailhead for Flint Ridge. The Klamath, second only to the Sacramento River in size of California rivers, winds 260 miles from eastern Oregon to its broad mouth. The Klamath River has the largest runs of salmon and steelhead in the state, making it a popular destination for sport fishermen. In fact, the banks near the mouth of the river have several resorts catering to anglers.

The Klamath was the heart of Yurok culture. Three dozen Yurok villages lay along the lower 40 miles of the river. The influence of the river was so great upon the culture that the Yurok language expresses directions in terms of upstream and downstream rather than the cardinal points used by most cultures. Today many Yuroks live on the Hoopa Valley Indian Reservation, which lies along the river.

After gold was discovered at Gold Bluffs in 1850, prospectors invaded the Klamath, taking much of the Yuroks' land. The forty-niners established the town of Klamath in 1851. The original town, located on the south bank near here, clustered around an iron house that provided protection when angry natives raided the invaders. The town lasted only a year before the gold seekers moved elsewhere.

Later another settlement called Klamath grew across the river. A ferry shuttled travelers for a fee until the Douglas Memorial Bridge opened in 1926. The original bridge and the town of Klamath were destroyed by the 1964 flood. The south portal of the old bridge, marked by two golden grizzly bears, is north of the parking area.

The trail descends northeast into a dense forest of red alders, then turns left to cross a bridge over Richardson Creek. Your trail parallels the creek, heading upstream to Marshall Pond. The trail veers right and follows the shore of this old mill pond. Keep an eye out for gnawed logs, a sign of the beavers living in the pond. Sometimes if you sit quietly at the pond's northeast corner (around ¼ mile), you will see a beaver break the surface of the still waters. But be forewarned: it takes patience, silence and luck.

After veering away from the pond, you meet a gravel road. This promptly makes two left turns, bringing you to a trail sign directing you back toward the pond. You follow its northern shore west on the old road. Climb gradually above the shore, passing a piece of old mill machinery at ½ mile.

Just before ¾ mile, your narrowing path suddenly switches right and climbs away from the pond. Climb into the dense forest, crossing a bridge over a tiny creek. Redwood sorrel, wild ginger, salal, huckleberry, and deer and sword ferns blanket the forest floor.

After another bridge, you climb by several switchbacks into a forest of larger redwoods mixed with Douglas firs. The trail steepens at one mile, climbing by many switchbacks toward Flint Ridge. After more bridges and some steps, you turn north at 1¾ miles and continue a steady but gradual climb through the dense redwood forest.

Just before 2 miles, the trail turns left as it gains the ridge top. You get a glimpse of the deep Klamath River Canyon to the north. Then climb southwest with the ridge. Redwoods here range to 12 feet in diameter, but most of the trees have broken tops, being exposed to harsh coastal winds that roar in at the mouth of the Klamath.

Your trail winds near the top of the ridge, with short up and down stretches. After 2½ miles a very steep drop lies on your left, with Richardson Creek far below. You stay south of the ridge top. The trail passes under a big fallen log at 2¾ miles. You descend to 3 miles, passing between a leaning fir and a rock outcrop.

Continue your winding descent to 3¼ miles. Then your trail levels as alders start to mix with the virgin redwood forest. You ascend to a second summit at 3¾ miles. Now alders dominate the forest; the sounds of pounding surf rise from 850 feet below.

At 3⅞ miles your trail switches left and descends by a series of switchbacks toward the coast. The vegetation becomes more lush; buttercup, coltsfoot and yellow skunk cabbage grow along the trail. Lichens droop from the alders.

Your steady descent brings you under a power line at 4¼ miles. In 250 feet the side trail to Flint Ridge Campground branches right. Ten sites in a grassy clearing provide tables, metal food lockers, water and a composting toilet.

Continue your descent north to cross a boardwalk at 4⅜ miles. The trail climbs briefly before it descends and switches left. You cross another bridge and come to a side road at 4½ miles, where a trail sign posts the distances in the opposite direction. You turn right and make a short descent to the western trailhead on the Coastal Drive.

7.

COASTAL DRIVE AND SHORT TRAILS
DRIVE/WALK A WILD COAST

The Coastal Drive hugs a rugged, steep section of coast between the mouth of the Klamath River and the north edge of Prairie Creek Redwoods State Park. The road provides the only opportunity (other than by boat) to see this wild stretch of coast. The drive is described from north to south.

Exit Highway 101 onto Klamath Beach Road, which follows the south bank of the broad river. In 1½ miles from the highway, you come to Alder Camp Road and the parking area for the Flint Ridge Trail (see Trail #6). Vehicles with trailers should turn left on Alder Camp Road, bypassing the narrow, steep and winding portion of Klamath Beach Road.

Continuing along Klamath Beach Road, you wind along the flat on the south side of the river, passing several seasonal fishing resorts and campgrounds. Immediately after the road starts to climb above the river flat, you come to South Klamath Overlook, 3.5 miles from Highway 101. From here you have a view of the mouth of the river. Nearby, Dad's Camp controls access to the gated road to the beach. To drive to the beach, you must pay $2.50 at Dad's. (It is $2 for seniors, less to walk in.) You can walk a mile north to the river mouth or, depending on the tide, up to 1½ miles south at the base of steep bluffs.

The gravel road climbs the steep, twisting grade. At 4

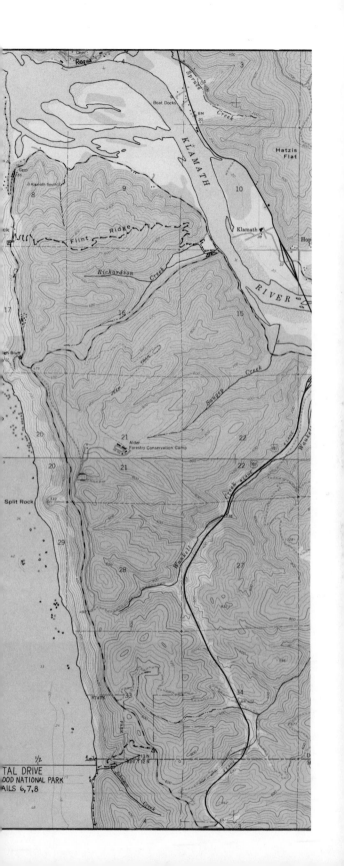

Requa

Boat Docks

BM
20

Hatzis
Flat

Gem

Klamath South

8

9

Klamath

10

Flint Ridge

Richardson Creek

Klamath

Hop

RIVER

17

16

15

h Bluff

TRAIL

Saugn Creek

20

21

Alder
Forestry Conservation Camp

22

Waukell

20

21

22

Split Rock

533

Creek Trail

29

28

Waukell

27

STATE

33

34

FGR

1/2   1mile   43N712N

TAL DRIVE
OOD NATIONAL PARK
AILS 6, 7, 8

COASTAL DRIVE AND SHORT TRAILS:

DISTANCE: Road is 9 miles long.
  Klamath beach access: 1-5 miles.
  Radar station trail: ¼ mile round trip.
  High Bluff trail: ½ mile round trip.
TIME: At least one hour.
TERRAIN: Road follows the Klamath River to its mouth, then climbs to high bluffs overlooking a wild and isolated coast. You return to the redwood forest before coming back to Highway 101.
ELEVATION GAIN/LOSS: Radar station trail: 40 feet+/-
  High Bluff trail: 120 feet-/120 feet+
BEST TIME: On a clear day; when it's foggy, you do not see much here. Spring for wildflowers.
WARNINGS: Drive carefully on the winding, occasionally steep road. No trailers allowed on Klamath Beach Road west of Alder Camp Road. Watch for poison oak when walking coastal grasslands.
DIRECTIONS TO TRAILHEAD: Exit Highway 101 onto Klamath Beach Road at M.3.7 (Del Norte) from the south, M.3.8 (Del Norte) from the north.
FEES: Klamath Beach access at Dad's Camp: $2.50/carload ($2 for seniors, less for walk-in).
FURTHER INFO: Redwood National Park (707) 464-6101; Dad's Camp (707) 482-3415.

miles from the highway, you come to the parking area for the west end of the Flint Ridge Trail. From here you can look down to the 175-foot pinnacle of Flint Rock Head on the sandy beach below. It is just a ¼-mile walk to the Flint Ridge Primitive Campground, where water is available.

At 4.3 miles on the road, you come to a wide spot where a trail descends to a World-War-II-vintage radar station in ⅛ mile. The station was disguised as a typical coastal ranch house to fool possible invaders from the Pacific.

Continuing along the Coastal Drive, at 5 miles you come to another short trail on your right. The trail descends northwest on an old road, then bends left and heads south to an old quarry at ¼ mile. From the spot marked "High Bluff" on the map, you look down a sheer cliff to the crashing breakers 300 feet below. From here, if it is clear enough, you have one of the best views of the rugged coast to the south, all the way to Patrick's Point (25 miles).

Just one mile south stands the massive rock outcrop

called Split Rock, sacred to the Yuroks. Composed of metamorphosed volcanic rock called greenstone, it rises 533 feet from the Pacific. Traditional Yurok belief held that rock outcrops were the last dwelling places of immortals on this earth. Although you cannot see it from here, Split Rock has a 100-foot-deep cleft down the middle. Yurok legend says that an ancestral fisherman anchored his net on the rock. Then the Spirit of the West Wind filled the net with an enormous catch of salmon, splitting the rock in two.

Just .1 mile beyond the High Bluff trail, Klamath Beach Road ends at Alder Camp Road. Turn right to continue the Coastal Drive. A turnout with a view of Split Rock is at 5.1 miles. At 6.7 and 6.9 miles, two more turnouts provide views of the precipitous coast 550 feet below.

Another turnout is 7.25 miles from the highway. A steep, short trail descends to an eagle's perch with spectacular views of the coast. Continuing south along the rough, roller-coaster drive, you come to yet another turnout at 7.7 miles. This one, with a sturdy stone wall, is known as Carruthers Cove Overlook. It features fine, bird's-eye views from an elevation of 600 feet south to Carruthers Cove, Ossagon Rocks, and Gold Bluffs Beach, and north to Split Rock.

You come to the trailhead for Carruthers Cove at 8.2 miles (see Trail #8). You then cross the boundary into Prairie Creek Redwoods State Park and turn inland, immediately coming to large redwoods. The road brings you back to Highway 101 after one more mile.

41

PRAIRIE CREEK
REDWOODS STATE PARK

On a moonlit night in Prairie Creek Campground, the silhouette of the land takes quintessential wilderness form. The tall forest parades atop the rolling ridges and along the very edge of the glistening, dewy prairie. The distant crashing of waves punctuates the profound silence, joined sometimes by the howl of a coyote, the piercing cry of a night bird, the crackle of a campfire, the soft crunching of elk grazing.

Prairie Creek Redwoods State Park comprises 12,544 acres of friendly wilderness (except when the weather turns fierce). Somehow nature graced it with an absence of the bane of hikers, poison oak. Its charms include vast virgin forests, verdant canyons with crystalline streams, herds of magnificent elk, and a wild, rugged coast of cliffs, waterfalls, wildflower-dappled dunes and gold-flecked beaches extending for miles. It is one of my favorite places on earth.

By the mid-1990s this paradise will become even better. The busy highway bisecting the park will turn into a sleepy country road when a new freeway opens east of the park.

8.

CARRUTHERS COVE
SECLUDED BEACH BACKED BY SPECTACULAR ROCKS

While the Coastal Drive provides spectacular views of the rugged shoreline south of the Klamath River's mouth at almost every turnout, the only trail down to this "Little Lost Coast" is the Carruthers Cove Trail. It leaves the Coastal Drive about a mile from the road's south end, right near the national park boundary sign. The steep, well-graded trail drops nearly 600 feet in ¾ mile to reach a pristine, driftwood-strewn beach with large rocks at the mouth of Johnson

CARRUTHERS COVE:

DISTANCE: .8 mile to beach, 1.6 miles round trip.
   To Butler Creek Backpack Camp: 4 miles one way.
TIME: One hour minimum.
TERRAIN: Descend steeply through alder/spruce forest to
   small cove on isolated stretch of beach. Walk south is on
   sand and may be impassable at high tide.
ELEVATION GAIN/LOSS: Round trip: 560 feet-/560 feet+
BEST TIME: Low tide. Marvelous for sunsets. Anytime OK.
WARNINGS: Watch for poison oak in the tangle of coastal
   vegetation near the beach. No camping here. Do not
   walk south more than ½ mile from the rocks when the
   tide is rising, or you may be cut off. Watch for oversize
   waves as you walk on the beach.
DIRECTIONS TO TRAILHEAD: Turn west off Highway 101
   at M.134.2 onto Coastal Drive. Trailhead is beside the
   sign marking the entrance to Redwood National Park
   lands, 0.95 miles from the highway.
FURTHER INFO: Prairie Creek Redwoods State Park (707)
   488-2171.
OTHER SUGGESTION: Can be used as a portion of the
   continuous Coastal Trail: after the Flint Ridge Section,
   walk south along the mostly gravel Coastal Drive. Then
   take Carruthers Cove Trail (at low tide) to join the Beach
   Trail (see Trail #15) at the mouth of Butler Creek.

*Creek. Unless it is high tide, you can walk south to Ossagon
Creek and the north end of Gold Bluffs Beach.*

*Though the trail is highly recommended, keep in mind
that the steep climb out will be the hardest part.*

The trail takes a few steep steps to drop onto the old roadbed
that you follow to the beach. You then head generally west
on the broad old road, descending through mixed Sitka
spruce and alder forest with a lush green understory. The
forest obscures all views of the coast as you curve right, then
bend left until you are heading southwest at ¼ mile.

Continue your steady descent toward the beach. Approaching the ½-mile point, your trail twists west, then
south before returning to a southwest bearing. You get a
glimpse of the coastline to the north through the dense
forest. Its full grandeur, however, still lies hidden.

Your trail steepens, approaching the ⅝-mile point. Swing
broadly left, getting your first good look at the beach below.

43

You soon bend left again, paralleling the deep canyon of Johnson Creek. Notice how the winds have sculpted the forest below.

Soon your trail switches sharply to the right. Descend west above the canyon, heading toward the beach. At ¾ mile you enter a clearing where you can see the mouth of the creek beyond the bramble thicket below.

In 300 feet your trail makes a sharp right, coming to your first clear view of the magnificent rock outcrop at the mouth of the creek. Then plunge steeply to the beach by a series of short switchbacks. This stretch of trail offers occasionally precarious footing, so proceed with caution. At the base of the switchbacks, make your way over a pile of driftwood. You reach firm footing on the beach sand at ⅞ mile.

It is ⅛ mile south across level, sand-filled Carruthers Cove to the base of the spectacular rock outcrops. Sea rocket and salal hunker beneath the imposing cliff. A crevice at the base of these rocks shelters you from the wind. You can snack or picnic here. Previous visitors have built driftwood fires in the shelter of the rock, but camping is not allowed. It is well worth a rest to contemplate the wild isolation of this coast.

To the north and south, the pristine beach stretches along the base of steep cliffs. Less than ¾ mile north, the sandy beach ends at the base of a rocky cliff. Just 2 miles north stands imposing Split Rock, rising 533 feet from the edge of the sea. This greenstone dome has a shape reminiscent of Yosemite's Half Dome when viewed from here.

If the tide is below +3.0 feet and ebbing, you can walk

south along the beach to the mouth of Ossagon Creek and beyond. It is ⅛ mile south to the tallest of several offshore rocks, a pointed spire. From the 1⅛-mile point, the beach gradually narrows. After 1⅜ miles you pass medium- to large-sized rocks scattered along the tide line. At 1⅝ miles you come to the crucial narrow spot, which is impassable at high tide. Here you must scramble around a protruding rock outcrop that is somewhat protected from large waves by the tall rocks offshore. You then hop over a thigh-high rock ledge, after which the beach becomes wider again. At 1¾ miles you pass another narrow spot, but it is nothing compared to the first one.

Continue south on the broadening beach. Tracks of elk, raccoon and occasionally mountain lion may be seen in the fine sand. Keep an eye out for the herd of elk that grazes Gold Bluffs Beach; they are frequently seen this far north. At 2¼ miles from your trailhead, you come to the Ossagon Rocks, which are on the beach as well as offshore. Go another ¼ mile and you are west of the place where the Ossagon Trail comes down to the coastal plain. You can head east to find the trail, which is marked by a sign where it rises from the flat beside Ossagon Creek. If you loop back on the Ossagon Trail, be sure to have arranged a car shuttle to return you to the Carruthers Cove Trailhead. If you head south along the Beach Trail, it is 3 miles to Fern Canyon and the roadend, 4¼ miles to the hike/bike camp at Gold Bluffs Beach.

9.

OSSAGON TRAIL
OLD ROAD TO HEART OF WILDERNESS BEACH

This trail follows an old road through redwood, spruce and alder forest. It makes a steep but short descent to the wildest portion of Gold Bluffs Beach, passing sites of an old homestead and a Yurok village. At the shore it meets the Beach Trail, which goes south to the Butler Creek, Boat Creek and Fern Canyon Trailheads. If you time your visit with the tides, you can also walk north to Carruthers Cove.

The trail climbs south-southwest from the highway amidst large redwoods. The old roadbed climbs steeply at first, then more gradually as you head west. An old bronze plaque beside the road marks a memorial grove.

Your trail levels at ⅛ mile as the roar of the surf overtakes the roar of traffic on the highway. You then climb gradually again to ¼ mile where large Sitka spruce mingle with the redwoods. One last easy uphill stretch brings you to ⅜ mile.

45

OSSAGON:

DISTANCE: 1.7 miles to beach (3.4 miles round trip). 4⅜ miles to Fern Canyon Trailhead.

TIME: At least 2 hours.

TERRAIN: Descend old road through forest to beach.

ELEVATION GAIN/LOSS: To beach: 120 feet+/720 feet- Round trip: 840 feet+/840 feet-.

BEST TIME: Winter, spring.

WARNINGS: Do not approach wild elk on beach. Mountain bikers: please stay on designated route and watch for hikers.

DIRECTIONS TO TRAILHEAD: Trail leaves directly from west side of Highway 101 at M.132.87. Better parking just south at parking area for Hope Creek Trail at M.132.74.

FURTHER INFO: Prairie Creek Redwoods State Park (707) 488-2171.

OTHER SUGGESTION: A MOUNTAIN BIKE LOOP has been designated that allows exploration of the park's back-country by bike. Total distance is 17½ miles. No other trails at Prairie Creek are open to biking. From the park entrance, bike north on Highway 101 for 5¾ miles. Then go west for 1¾ miles on the Ossagon Trail. At the beach, head south on the Beach Trail for 3 miles. Then follow Gold Bluffs Road for 4½ miles to its summit, where you meet the Jogging Trail. Take this for 2 miles, then complete the loop with ½ mile on the campground road.

You now start a steady descent toward the coast. The road makes a big bend to the right, descending steeply. As your trail bends back to the left, a stand of immense redwoods lines the path. These quickly give way to a forest of alders as you descend southwest. The trail turns west at ½ mile. You can glimpse the ocean through the trees, though the view is best in winter when the alders have dropped their leaves.

At ⅝ mile the trail bends left, then back to the right. Evergreen violets grow in the roadbed. You continue to descend steadily, wrapping around another big bend. At ⅞ mile your trail makes another big bend to the right, approaching a crossing of Ossagon Creek at one mile. A grassy clearing on the left marks the site of an old homestead.

Descend to cross the creek on a sturdy bridge. You then climb 20 steps to return to the roadbed. The trail stays

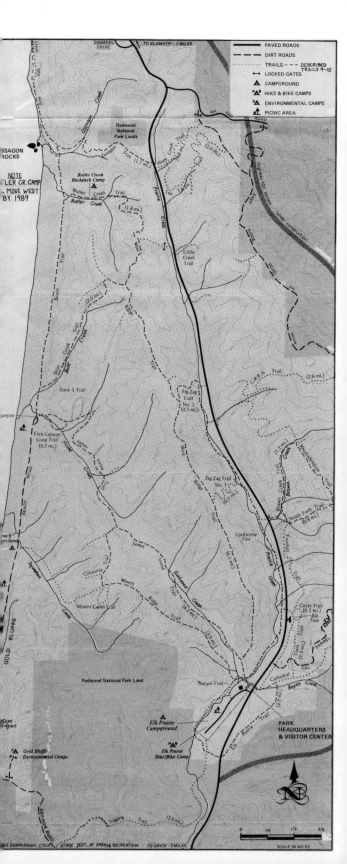

mostly level to 1⅜ miles. As you descend again, you can see the broad beach ahead. On your right is Ossagon Prairie, once the site of the small Yurok hamlet of Osegen. Several side trails lead up to the large, steeply sloping prairie with a pleasant southern exposure.

The main trail descends steeply from here, passing two overgrown side trails on the right. At the second of these, the old road turns sharply left and makes its last descent to level beside Ossagon Creek. (A sign at the base of the hill marks the trail back to the highway.) You are 1½ miles from the trailhead.

A faint trail leads northwest from this spot, though it quickly becomes overgrown and hard to follow, leading into a swampy area. You should follow the main trail southwest to a crossing of the creek in ⅛ mile. Notice the elk wallow just downstream from the crossing. On the other side of the creek you leave the alder forest for flat coastal prairie. Keep your eyes open for the herd of elk that frequents this area.

The main trail leads south to the Butler Creek Trail in ½ mile. It is 2¾ miles to Fern Canyon Trailhead. You can also go north on the beach to Carruthers Cove if the tide is +3.0 feet or lower. It is 1¾ miles to where that trail comes down to the beach (see Trail #8).

To get to the beach from the creek crossing, you can either follow the meandering creek to its outlet or take a shorter route. For the latter, a well-beaten path leads west from the creek crossing. The tread gets more sandy after ⅛ mile, as Ossagon Rocks come into view to the north. You then come to a second crossing of the creek. The water is deeper here. You may have to construct a makeshift bridge from nearby driftwood. On the other side of the creek, you can head due west to the breakers or turn north and head for the western-most of the Ossagon Rocks. If you are heading north, be sure the rising tide does not cut off your return.

Leave ample time before sunset to hike back to the trail-head. One hour should be sufficient.

BROWN CREEK/RHODODENDRON SOUTH FORK LOOP

PRIMEVAL FOREST ON A BABBLING BROOK

The Brown Creek Trail provides a rewarding break for travelers to stretch their legs before continuing along Highway 101. The trail, built in 1951, is just long enough and steep enough to stimulate your tight muscles. Its spectacular, pristine beauty will stretch your eyes, mind and imagination as well. One of the park's most beautiful hikes at any time of the year, it will reward you in spring with a dazzling array of rhododendrons and other wildflowers.

You can stroll up Brown Creek and return by the same trail for an easy 2½-mile (or less) round trip. Or you can follow the loop exactly as described for a steeper 3½-mile loop. If you want a longer hike, continue south on the Rhododendron Trail beyond the South Fork Trail. If you have a driver to pick you up where the trail crosses Cal Barrel Road, the hike is about 3¾ miles. If you continue to the end of the Rhododendron Trail and loop back on the Foothill Trail or the Prairie Creek Trail (across the highway), the distance is 8 or 8½ miles. Whichever option you take, your entire hike will be in primeval redwood forest.

The Brown Creek Trail heads east from Highway 101, climbing into mature redwood forest. Almost immediately you come upon an immense redwood with a flared base more than 17 feet in diameter. You then reach a spot overlooking Brown Creek before you descend into primeval forest alongside the creek.

At ⅛ mile you come to a junction where the Foothill Trail goes right. The Brown Creek Trail continues straight, promptly crossing a boardwalk. You hike up the beautiful canyon, following Brown Creek. At ¼ mile a second boardwalk is slippery and 100 feet long. After another boardwalk, you are back beside the creek. You stay near it until ⅜ mile, where you veer left through a tunnel under immense fallen logs.

The forest consists of redwoods of varying shapes and sizes. Its understory is jammed with deer and sword ferns, redwood sorrel and salal. In March and April, trilliums abound, and you may see delicate calypso orchids. In May or June, the shocking pink blooms of rhododendrons splash the forest with color.

Your trail winds through the forest, but you never lose the sound of the murmuring stream. After ½ mile you descend

BROWN CREEK/RHODODENDRON
SOUTH FORK LOOP:

DISTANCE: 3½-mile loop with options for an 8- or 8½-mile loop.

TIME: 2-4 hours.

TERRAIN: Up a canyon of primeval redwood forest, climbing to a ridge, then descending the ridge to your starting point.

ELEVATION GAIN/LOSS: 675 feet+/675 feet-

BEST TIME: Spring for wildflowers, late afternoon for best lighting.

DIRECTIONS TO TRAILHEAD: On east side of Highway 101 at M.129.2, 2 miles north of main park entrance. Parking on either side of highway.

FURTHER INFO: Prairie Creek Redwoods State Park (707) 488-2171.

OTHER SUGGESTION: You can drive CAL BARREL ROAD to the upper portion of the RHODODENDRON TRAIL. Turn east off Highway 101 at M.127.5. At 1.8 miles you cross the Rhododendron Trail. You can hike south 2¼ miles to the Cathedral Trees Trail, or north for 4 miles to its end at the CREA Trail. You can also bike Cal Barrel Road.

briefly before climbing along the creek again. Iris and huckleberry are prolific here.

After ⅝ mile you come to a spur trail. It crosses Brown Creek and enters the Trees of the Great Grove, dedicated to Carl Schenck, founder of America's first school of forestry. To this great forester is attributed a wonderful quote: "Forestry is a great thing but love is better." It took much love and energy (not to mention money) to save the virgin forests of Prairie Creek.

Your trail stays near the creek, climbing gradually to another grove of immense redwood giants. This one is dedicated to Frederick Olmstead, co-founder of the Save-the-Redwoods League and designer of New York's Central Park.

Continue up the canyon, crossing a short boardwalk at ⅞ mile. Before one mile, two short downhill stretches bring you to more boardwalks. A steep downhill brings you back beside the creek at 1⅛ miles. You climb briefly to meet the junction with the Rhododendron Trail.

Now you must make your decision. For the shortest hike, retrace your steps to Highway 101 (2½ miles round trip). Either direction you take on the Rhododendron Trail climbs steeply out of Brown Creek Canyon, gaining 300 to 350 feet in elevation in ½ mile. Our described route heads south on the Rhododendron Trail.

You cross a bridge over Brown Creek, then climb moderately. At 1¼ miles the trail wraps around an immense redwood with a huge fire scar on its back side. You climb southeast, with views back into the canyon. The climb becomes steeper around 1½ miles. After 1¾ miles your trail levels briefly, providing a break from the steep climb. The trail narrows through a brushy area. You come to a dedicated grove of redwoods at 1⅞ miles. Large sword ferns cover every inch of ground. The distant roar of surf drifts through the silent forest.

Just before 2 miles, you duck under a fallen tree. The mostly level trail winds along the side of a steep hill. Many rhododendrons grow here, as well as an abundance of huckleberries. Descend to cross two small streams, then climb by several short, steep switchbacks to a junction atop a ridge at 2½ miles.

For a 3½-mile loop, you turn right and descend the South Fork Trail. Those wanting a longer hike can continue south along the Rhododendron Trail. It climbs 120 feet to its 960-foot summit in ½ mile. Then it descends to cross Cal Barrel Road (1.2 miles from here) and drops steeply to Boyes Creek, connecting with the Cathedral Trees, Elk Prairie and Foothill Trails.

The South Fork Trail descends steeply along a ridge. Redwoods, rhododendrons, redwood sorrel, trilliums and huckleberries thrive here. Your trail steepens at 2¾ miles and descends by numerous switchbacks. The trail finally levels, crossing a bridge over the South Fork of Brown Creek. After a short level stretch, you meet the Foothill Trail at 3¼ miles.

Turn right onto the Foothill Trail and descend steeply. You promptly come to another bridge that crosses back over the South Fork. You then walk a rickety old raised boardwalk through a swampy area. At 3⅜ miles you cross a quaint old bridge over the main fork of Brown Creek to meet the Brown Creek Trail. Turn left, and you will be back at your starting point in ⅛ mile.

11

WEST RIDGE
PRAIRIE CREEK LOOP
RIDGE, FOREST AND CREEK

The West Ridge Trail traverses the backbone of Prairie Creek Redwoods State Park. You can use it for a moderately short but varied day hike by looping back on the Zig Zag Trail #1 (6 miles), a longer loop day hike with the Zig Zag #2 (8⅝ miles), or an overnight backpack (15 miles or more). All three choices offer the solitude and silence of virgin forest. If you choose the overnight option, you can leave your car securely parked by the Visitor Center and spend a weekend or a week exploring the backcountry. Be sure to register at park headquarters.

Butler Creek Backpack Camp nestles in the heart of the park's roadless area. The wilderness beach, a herd of elk, steep-walled canyons, virgin forests, the site of an Indian village, and more lie within a mile of camp. Here you can feel far removed from civilization, though you are just one mile from busy Highway 101 as the crow flies.

Your trail starts at the Visitor Center, where you can inquire about current trail conditions and get a camping permit if you are staying at Butler Creek Camp. You follow the Nature Trail for just over ⅛ mile, then go right on the Irvine Trail, which heads north. Just beyond ¼ mile from your starting point, you meet the West Ridge Trail on your right. Take this trail heading east-northeast.

You climb steadily by many short switchbacks to gain the ridge at ⅝ mile. The virgin forest stretches in all directions. Redwoods of 15 feet in diameter grow beside the trail. Continue climbing, with occasional switchbacks. Your trail levels briefly after ¾ mile, then begins a more gradual climb. Douglas firs mingle with the redwoods in this drier habitat. Climb steeply again, then descend briefly to one mile. The roar of traffic from the nearby highway is softened by the forest.

From 1⅛ miles your trail follows the ridgetop which rolls up and down through the forest. Leather ferns grow on a redwood to the left. You climb intermittently to 1½ miles where the top of the ridge becomes broad and level. Redwoods grow to 16 feet in diameter here.

The ridge soon narrows. Your trail climbs again, reaching an 800-foot peak on the ridge at 2 miles, the highest point in the first 5 miles. Descend briefly, then level, winding along the ridgetop. You pass a grove with a rest bench on the right.

WEST RIDGE/PRAIRIE CREEK LOOP:

DISTANCE: 12.2-mile loop.
TIME: Full day.
TERRAIN: Up to and along a ridge in virgin redwood forest,
    returning along the creek.
ELEVATION GAIN/LOSS: 1730 feet+/1730 feet-
    Including Butler Creek Camp: 2130 feet+/2130 feet-
BEST TIME: Spring.
WARNINGS: No camping in backcountry, except in desig-
    nated camps.
DIRECTIONS TO TRAILHEAD: Turn west off Highway 101
    at M.127.1, the main entrance to Prairie Creek Red-
    woods State Park. Trail starts from Visitor Center.
FEES: $3 day use/parking ($2 for seniors). Backcountry
    camping is $2 per person per night.
FURTHER INFO: Prairie Creek Redwoods State Park (707)
    488-2171

Climb by short switchbacks to 2¼ miles, then descend to a low notch in the ridge. At 2⅝ miles you meet Zig Zag Trail #1, which descends east to the Prairie Creek Trail. You can turn right and return to your starting point for a 6-mile loop.

West Ridge Trail heads northwest, quickly coming to the comfortable rest bench of Forever Grove. You descend slightly, then climb with intermittent level stretches, heading northwest. Pass a stand of coast hemlock and Douglas fir, then make a short, easy descent to 3 miles. The sound of the surf drifts in from the west.

You continue along the top of the ridge, ascending and descending with the rolling terrain. At 3⅜ miles from your trailhead, two switchbacks drop you to a low saddle. You climb to 3¾ miles then meet the junction with the Zig Zag Trail #2. Day hikers can turn east here, descending to the Prairie Creek Trail in ½ mile and following Prairie Creek south to the trailhead for an 8¾-mile loop.

After the junction, the West Ridge Trail turns sharply left and heads west along the ridge. The trail is mostly level to 4⅛ miles. The next section of trail has a series of short, steep ups and downs. At 4⅝ miles you climb to a high point that has been marred by a fire.

In 1987 a hiker camped here illegally, then lit a fire inside the goose pen of the scorched redwood on the right. The fire roared to ignite the top of the tree and spread from there to the surrounding forest. This foolish act cost $100,000 and could have resulted in the tragic devastation of Prairie Creek's virgin forest. But fast-acting firefighters were able to extinguish the blaze without major damage. The charred giants stand as a dramatic reminder to be careful with fire.

Your level trail continues north, passing gnarled old redwoods in a forest mixed with Sitka spruce, Douglas fir and hemlock. After a short uphill stretch at 4¾ miles, the trail follows the ridgetop with its dense cover of brush, mostly salal and huckleberry. Then comes an area of dense conifer regeneration, towered over by redwood giants. You descend through a tunnel of young growth to meet a broad old road that you follow north.

At 5 miles a sign indicates that you are ½ mile from the Boat Creek Trail. You head north along a shady lane, passing a spur trail to Brown Grove on the left. You climb gradually northwest, then bend right, climbing steeply to meet the Boat Creek Trail at 5½ miles. The Boat Creek Trail heads west and follows the creek to its mouth (see Trail #15).

Continuing on the West Ridge Trail, you climb briefly to the 860-foot summit of the trail. You descend for the next ⅛ mile. Then your broad road climbs again, more gradually now, to just beyond 5¾ miles. You come to a big bend where a break in the forest provides views northwest to the mouth of Butler Creek Canyon and the blue Pacific. This is the most expansive view on the hike. You might want to take a break to appreciate it.

The West Ridge Trail now descends to its junction with the Butler Creek Trail just beyond 6 miles. West Ridge Trail turns east from here and descends to meet Highway 101 in just over ¼ mile. But the north portion of the Prairie Creek Trail is now closed, so that those hiking east to the highway must return on the shoulder of the busy road. Day hikers will do better to return south along West Ridge to Zig Zag Trail #2, take that trail to the Prairie Creek Trail, and head south from there.

Of course backpackers want to take the Butler Creek Trail. It makes a winding descent through the forest, coming to Butler Creek in 1¼ miles. In ⅛ mile you cross a side stream from the north, then come to Butler Creek Camp, 7⅜ miles from park headquarters.

A side trail on the right leads to Butler Creek Camp. Its 8 campsites have fire rings and pit toilets. Be sure to purify water from the stream. Please pack out all refuse. The campground lies ½ mile from the mouth of Butler Creek and the heart of Gold Bluffs Beach. Fine day hikes can be taken north or south along the beach (see Trails #8, 9 and 13), or you can just lie around camp and soak up the silence.

There are three great options for your return hike to park headquarters. You can take the Beach Trail south to Fern Canyon, then follow the James Irvine Trail southeast for a 7-mile return. Or you can return the way you came, hiking the length of the West Ridge Trail. Or you can follow the West Ridge Trail to the Zig Zag Trail #2 and complete your return via the latter and the beautiful Prairie Creek Trail, an 8⅝-mile return. This third option is described below.

Retrace your steps, ascending the Butler Creek Trail to West Ridge, then turning right and climbing south on the West Ridge Trail. You reach the 860-foot summit in only 1⅞ miles. Continue to retrace your steps along West Ridge to the junction with Zig Zag #2, 3¾ miles from Butler Camp.

For day hikers and backpackers alike, the return hike is described with the West Ridge/Zig Zag #2 junction as the starting or zero-mile point. Zig Zag #2 heads northeast, then turns east and descends by switchbacks, following a small creek. After ½ mile of moderately steep descent, your trail levels near Prairie Creek and makes a sharp right, coming to a rustic bridge. Cross the bridge, meeting the Prairie Creek Trail in 100 feet. Turn right and head south.

Before one mile an immense cluster of redwoods stands on the left of the trail. The circle of three trees partially grown together is about 30 feet in diameter. The trail meanders, following the many bends of Prairie Creek. At 1⅛ miles a big pool in the creek provides wading in summer.

Large Sitka spruce grow at 1¼ miles. Then you cross a series of five boardwalks. At 1⅜ miles you must duck under a log fallen across the trail. A spur trail forks right to Drury Grove. You continue south through another big clearing.

You meet the junction with Zig Zag Trail #1 at 1⅞ miles. At 2 miles your trail enters another large clearing. A big, beautiful pool lies beside the trail. You cross a sturdy bridge over the creek, immediately coming to a fork in the trail. Go right at the junction. In 200 feet a long, old, tilting bridge is right beside Highway 101. After crossing it, you head away from the highway to the other side of the canyon.

Continue through the forest, then back alongside the creek briefly. At 3½ miles you climb above the creek onto the cutbank of the canyon, with a pretty view of the creek below. You descend immediately to cross a bridge and return to the east bank. You climb up and over a huge log by steps, then pass Big Tree Trail on the left.

Continuing south on the Prairie Creek Trail, at 3⅞ miles a huge redwood overhangs a grassy clearing by the creek. The opening provides beautiful views of the creek for the next ⅛ mile. This is a good place to spot birds when you have the woods to yourself, or a good place to get your feet wet in summer. You stay near the creek until 4⅝ miles, where you climb some steps onto the cutbank. Your trail ducks under a large redwood root and meets the Nature Trail. You turn right, then take the next left to the trailhead at park headquarters before 5 miles.

12.

ELK PRAIRIE LOOP

STALKING THE MIGHTY ELK

About 200 Roosevelt elk (Cervus elaphus rooseveltii) live around Prairie Creek Redwoods. The elk is the second largest member of the deer family, smaller than the moose. Males grow up to 1100 pounds, stand four to five feet at the shoulder, and grow antlers five feet long, with a four- to six-foot spread at the tips.

Elk once inhabited much of Northern California. They were hunted nearly to extinction for their meat, hides and canine teeth (believed to bring good luck). Now protected from hunting in California, they range north to British Columbia and east to the Rockies.

Each March the bulls shed their antlers, growing up to 40 pounds of new antlers by August. As the mating season approaches in September, solitary bulls join the herd. Mature bulls compete for a harem of up to 40 cows. If you visit during mating season, you may hear the bugle-like call of the bull, followed by the clash of antlers as two bulls try to knock each other to their haunches. Consider yourself lucky if you get to see such a mating joust. Next May or June, some of the cows bear single calves weighing 25 to 40 pounds at birth that will grow to three-quarters of their adult size by fall.

Though the elk are primarily peaceful, grazing animals, they should never be approached on foot. Bulls especially may give chase if they feel threatened or cornered, charging at up to 35 miles per hour. They may look tame, but they are wild animals.

This description starts at the southwest corner of the campground, near campsite 67, one good place to start this loop. It circles Boyes Prairie, home to one of the park's three herds of elk, letting you view elk habitat first hand. Carry binoculars to observe the elk without getting too close.

Your trail heads south into a forest of alder and Sitka spruce. About ¼ mile you cross a small creek, then leave the forest for the open prairie, joining a spur trail from the hike/bike campsites. You follow an old road, soon parallel-

ELK PRAIRIE LOOP:

DISTANCE: 2¼-mile loop.

TIME: 1-2 hours.

TERRAIN: Mostly level across prairie, then slight up and down through the forest.

ELEVATION GAIN/LOSS: 100 feet+/100 feet-

BEST TIME: Spring for wildflowers. Anytime for elk.

WARNINGS: Elk are wild animals. Never approach them on foot. Use caution crossing Highway 101. Trail may be muddy in winter.

DIRECTIONS TO TRAILHEAD: Turn west off Highway 101 at M.127.1, the main entrance to Prairie Creek Redwoods State Park. Go south through campground to campsite #67, the starting point for this description. (You can also start from the Visitor Center.)

FEES: $3 day use/parking ($2 for seniors).

FURTHER INFO: Prairie Creek Redwoods State Park (707) 488-2171.

OTHER SUGGESTION: REVELATION TRAIL starts south of the Visitor Center, circling through a redwood grove for 1/3 mile. Wood and rope guide rails, tape recorders and signs allow the blind or otherwise disabled visitor to explore the forest independently.

PRAIRIE CREEK FISH HATCHERY, at M.124.72 on right of Highway 101, shows how salmon and steelhead are raised to restock local creeks. Open 8 to 4:30 daily.

ing a redwood split-rail fence.

At a break in the fence, the trail turns left and crosses the south end of Boyes Prairie. Heading toward the highway, watch for elk on the trail. If you find them, *be sure to make a wide detour around them.*

After a small bridge, you come to Highway 101 at ½ mile. Use extreme caution crossing the busy road. Pick up the trail on the other side at another bridge and head into a forest of hemlock, redwood and spruce. After climbing a short hill, your trail turns left and parallels the highway above the prairie.

Walking through the forest you will see many signs of elk: trees with bark rubbed off by bulls scraping their antlers; droppings and hoofprints along the trail; elk wallows, the depressions dug in the ground by hooves and antlers; munched deer ferns and branches stripped of their bark.

Your trail meanders gently up and down through the forest. At ⅝ mile the forest thins for a view of the prairie and perhaps a herd of elk. You pass large redwoods, including one with a base 16 feet in diameter. Large big leaf maples compete for sunlight at the border of the forest and prairie. California bay laurel, wild ginger, huckleberries and sword ferns grow along the trail.

At one mile you come to the first of several dilapidated bridges that have been trampled by the elk. Watch your step on the slippery, broken boards. You quickly come to a grove of large redwoods. At 1⅛ miles you pass a big redwood root ball, then parallel the fallen length of the tree for 300 feet.

At 1¼ miles, cross another small bridge, then an old service road behind some park residences. You pass several redwoods that were cut around 1900 to build the Boyes' houses and barn. At 1½ miles your trail passes through a dense berry thicket that towers overhead. After crossing a larger bridge, you come to a trail junction. The right fork leads to the Rhododendron and Cathedral Trees Trails.

The Elk Prairie Trail turns left and soon meets an arm of the prairie. You follow its border with the redwood forest. A rest bench looks over the beautiful grasslands. About 1⅝ miles you meet the start of the Foothill Trail, which goes north. Your trail turns left, crossing a bridge over Boyes Creek, then passing through a marsh.

At 1¾ miles you pass under the highway. Then follow the main park road past the entrance station and Visitor Center, returning to your starting point at campsite 67.

13.

JAMES IRVINE MINERS RIDGE LOOP

ROUTE OF 1851 GOLD SEEKERS

In spring 1850, five frustrated prospectors left the Klamath mines and headed for the coast. At the mouth of the Klamath River they turned south. Though always keeping their eyes open for gold, they perhaps were more enticed by stories of new settlements at Trinidad and Humboldt Bays south on the coast, places where one could find such rare amenities as hot baths, beds, women and fresh food. But after trekking another 10 rugged miles through virgin forests and steep terrain, their dreams of comfort were postponed. Near the mouth of Home Creek, Hermann Ehrenberg found fine gold dust mixed with coarse, dark sand on the beach. The prospectors hastily gathered samples, marked their claim, then continued their journey south.

JAMES IRVINE/MINERS RIDGE LOOP:

DISTANCE: James Irvine Trail: 4.3 miles, one way.
   Miners Ridge Trail: 3.9 miles, one way.
   Clintonia Trail: 1.0 mile, one way.
   Combined loop as described: 9¼ miles.

TIME: Minimum 4 hours. Best as full day with lunch.

TERRAIN: Along Godwood Creek through virgin forest, over
   a low summit and down Home Creek to mouth of Fern
   Canyon. On return, climb through more virgin forest to
   Miners Ridge, which you follow to your starting point.

ELEVATION GAIN/LOSS: Full loop: 1350 feet+/1350 feet-
   James Irvine Trail east to west: 350 feet+/490 feet-
   Round trip: 840 feet+/840 feet-

BEST TIME: Spring for wildflowers. June to September for
   footbridges in Fern Canyon. Still recommended: March
   through October.

WARNINGS: May be impassable November to February after
   big storms.

DIRECTIONS TO TRAILHEAD: Main entrance to Prairie
   Creek Redwoods on Highway 101 at M.127.1. Trail starts
   near Visitor Center.

FEES: $3 day use/parking ($2 for seniors).

FURTHER INFO: Prairie Creek Redwoods State Park (707)
   488-2171.

OTHER SUGGESTION: A different loop can be made by
   walking the Irvine Trail to its west end, then following
   the beach south one mile to the western Miners Ridge
   Trailhead and returning the full length of that trail. The
   first portion of the latter follows an old corduroy logging
   road. Distance: 9.1 miles.

*After another 25 miles of hard travel, they reached the
boomtown of Trinidad. That same year they organized the
Pacific Mining Company and began to develop their claim at
what came to be called Gold Bluffs and Gold Bluff Beach.*

*The gold was abundant when first found, though in the
form of the tiniest gold flakes imaginable. The principals of
the Pacific Mining Company, optimistic after their initial*

59

excavations, predicted a return of 43 million dollars for each member of the Company.

Word quickly spread among the settlers at Trinidad and Humboldt Bay. Only the arrival of harsh winter storms kept them from setting out immediately. But in the spring of 1851, thousands headed north to the Gold Bluffs. They left the recently established trail to the Klamath mines at Madison Prairie and headed west on a narrow track, known today as the James Irvine Trail. Arriving at Gold Bluffs, they rapidly built a tent city in a clearing above the beach.

The boom was short-lived, however. Retrieving the gold required labor- and machine-intensive methods only a few were patient and resourceful enough to pursue. Although thousands of dollars in gold were eventually recovered, the boom tent city quickly dwindled to a small company mining camp. Still, the Irvine Trail remained the main route to the gold fields, being used extensively during the Civil War, when gold was at a premium, and again in the 1870s, as two other companies tried to succeed. In the end Gold Bluffs mining may have produced more debts than gold.

Today the explorers come for different reasons: to see the magnificent virgin forest, to revel in nature's quiet, and to explore the non-negotiable treasure of Fern Canyon.

To walk the James Irvine Trail west to Fern Canyon and Gold Bluffs, take the Nature Trail from the Visitor Center. You cross a sturdy bridge over Prairie Creek and pass the start of the Prairie Creek Trail, just 500 feet from your starting point (see Trail #11). Then the trail meanders toward the creek until the James Irvine Trail branches right, ⅛ mile from your trailhead. The Irvine Trail heads north, climbing gradually to the West Ridge Trail junction at ¼ mile.

The Irvine Trail runs northwest, following the gentle drainage of Godwood Creek, named for an early homesteader. Ancient redwoods stand along the trail. Some reach diameters of 18 feet. The virgin forest is a mix of redwood, Sitka spruce, Douglas fir and occasional hardwoods like tanoak and maple. At ½ mile you are alongside Godwood Creek.

The well-beaten trail continues mostly level through the primeval forest. Watch out for roots that disrupt the surface of the trail. Also watch your footing on the corduroy bridges; they are slippery when wet. At ¾ mile you cross a sturdy bridge, then walk a recently-built boardwalk spanning a marshy area. Salal, piggyback plant, skunk cabbage, sword and deer ferns thrive here.

After two more corduroy bridges, you pass the one-mile point. You cross many more corduroy bridges as you climb gradually toward the summit. At 1¼ miles you cross Godwood Creek on a sturdy bridge, putting you on its west side. At 1⅝ miles you cross the creek twice more, finally leaving it as its headwaters swing northeast.

At 1¾ miles you pass through a blowdown area. Many fallen trees lie along and across the trail here, prey to ferocious winds. At 2 miles you come to a rest bench carved from a fallen log, beyond which another fallen log spans the trail at head height. Don't forget to duck! At 2⅛ miles you cross a dilapidated boardwalk.

The trail winds around an immense redwood with a swollen base of 16 feet. It marks the halfway point to the beach. You cross a small gully, then climb to the summit of the Irvine Trail, at the elevation of 300 feet.

You descend slightly to the Clintonia Trail at 2⅜ miles. It leads to the Miners Ridge Trail, described in the return portion of this hike.

The Irvine Trail descends gradually, then more rapidly by rough steps. At 2¾ miles you cross a bridge over the headwaters of Home Creek. The trail then levels before passing under two fallen logs, after which a series of short ups and downs brings you to a bridge over a side canyon at 3 miles. Beyond the bridge, a side trail leads to a grove on this quiet side stream.

The vegetation becomes more dense as you approach the coast. Deer ferns, red and evergreen huckleberries and delicate redwood violets thrive here. Follow the sound of a waterfall down to another bridge, this one over a 50-foot-deep canyon lush with ferns. After the bridge is another grove spur trail.

From 3⅛ miles you meander up and down the slope above

Home Creek, crossing more corduroy bridges. At 3½ miles a very large Sitka spruce sits on the left, on the edge of upper Fern Canyon. The trail is mostly level before you descend to cross a beautiful canyon at 3⅝ miles. Baldwin Bridge has a lovely bench overlooking the gorge.

You soon pass the junction with the Zone 5 Loop Trail. After crossing a small bridge at 3¾ miles you again approach Fern Canyon. But you must hike another ½ mile before meeting the trail into the canyon. On this fairly level stretch, notice a Sitka spruce on your left growing atop a fallen redwood. The other end of the Zone 5 Trail is on your right.

About 4¼ miles from the trailhead, you meet the upper end of the Fern Canyon Trail. You may descend into the canyon here, or walk the Irvine Trail to the beach and return by way of Fern Canyon. Our description follows the Irvine Trail to its end. The trail descends steps through alder forest. On your left is the Alexander Lincoln Prairie, the site of the Gold Bluffs tent city of the 1850s, now with no hint of its strange history. Descend more steps, follow a 100-foot boardwalk, and drop to the beach, just north of the mouth of Fern Canyon.

For a total loop of 9½ miles, you can walk south 1½ miles on the beach, then return the full length of the Miners Ridge Trail.

Our described loop follows Trail #14 through marvelous Fern Canyon to its junction with the Irvine Trail. Then retrace your steps east to the junction with the Clintonia Trail (1⅝ miles from the beach). If you want the shortest route back, continue to retrace your steps on the Irvine Trail.

If you are still game for new country, follow the Clintonia /Miners Ridge Loop described below. It requires only an extra ⅝ mile and an extra 500 feet in elevation gain and loss. Most of the extra climbing comes in the first ¼ mile. You start out steeply uphill, following a spur ridge up to Miners Ridge. You are rewarded with views on all sides down upon the virgin forest.

After a short level but winding stretch, you climb steeply again. In spring, watch for the bright red flowers of the clintonia on long stalks. In summer they bear dark-blue, inedible berries. Your trail levels, then descends a bit as you enter dense, young-growth forest. Where a spur trail forks right, you veer left into a dark tunnel of young growth.

At ½ mile you return to open virgin forest. Your trail remains mostly level, then descends to meet the Miners Ridge Trail where it climbs steeply from Squashan Creek. Right by the junction, the Miners Cabin Loop heads south.

Our route turns left to follow Miners Ridge back to the Visitor Center. Climb steeply until your trail levels along the ridge, passing huge fire-scarred redwoods. You climb to 1¼ miles. Continue up, down and level along the ridge, with grand views of the virgin forest.

At 1⅞ miles from Irvine Trail, notice the lack of big trees to the south. It is only ¼ mile to the park boundary. Though now national park land beyond, it was clearcut in the 1960s. At 2 miles you start to descend, gradually at first, and still with a few uphill stretches. To the north the Irvine Trail is less than ⅛ mile away, but far below. At 2⅝ miles you descend steeply and continuously.

You come to the junction with the Nature Trail at the 3-mile point, alongside Prairie Creek. Big leaf maples and alders grow in the canyon. In fall these deciduous trees provide brilliant splashes of gold and red in the otherwise verdant forest.

Go left at the junction. It is just ¼ mile to the Visitor Center and hike's end.

14.

FERN CANYON LOOP
FIFTY-FOOT WALLS OF FERNS

Known as the jewel of Prairie Creek Redwoods State Park, Fern Canyon nestles in the heart of Gold Bluffs Beach. Though its name is common along the fog-enshrouded North Coast, this one stands alone for its geology, history and singular beauty.

About four million years ago, the Klamath River emptied into the sea here. The river deposited gravels from the Klamath Mountains 40 miles to the east. Rough ocean waves washed and eroded these gravels for thousands of years until they were laid out in flat, uniform deposits. In more recent geologic times, Home Creek carved its way through these layers of gravel to create the canyon you see today. Its flat, level floor differs from the steep slopes of most North Coast streams.

The ancestral Klamath River also deposited the fine particles of gold that brought prospectors to the area from 1850 to the 1920s. The gold was so fine that much of it could not be separated from the tons of dark sand and gravel mixed with it. Mining activities peaked in the 1880s, when 300 people lived near Fern Canyon to work the gold deposits. Most of them lived on the Lincoln Prairie, a grassy clearing north of Fern Canyon. Today the signs of past mining and logging have vanished.

Coastal fog and an annual rainfall of 80 inches help to create the verdant, fern-filled habitat of Fern Canyon. The most common fern here is the five-finger fern, a relative of the maidenhair. The Yuroks gathered these ferns for the black stems with which they wove designs into their beautiful baskets. Other ferns grow in the canyon in less abundance: sword, lady, deer, woodwardia, California wood and leather. Less common but found occasionally are bladder, bracken and licorice ferns, nine species in all.

Other moisture-loving plants grow here: piggyback plant, common and tooth-leaved monkeyflower, coastal manroot, fairy lantern and twisted stalk. One of the most lethal plants in North America grows here, California water hemlock. As little as one centimeter of the plant can be fatal. The oenanthe is another poisonous plant commonly found in the canyon. Edible plants include salmonberry and thimbleberry.

Many water-loving animals call Fern Canyon home. The Pacific giant salamander lives in the still pools of Home Creek, feeding on banana slugs, bugs and mice. It is one of the largest North American salamanders, up to 10 inches long. Other amphibians include the rare tailed frog, the Olympic salamander and the more abundant western red-

---

FERN CANYON LOOP:

DISTANCE: ¾-mile loop.

TIME: 30 minutes, but it is worth taking more time or planning a picnic.

TERRAIN: Up the canyon floor beneath fifty-foot-high, fern-covered walls, then climbing out of the canyon into virgin forest and returning to its mouth.

ELEVATION GAIN/LOSS: 180 feet+/180 feet-

BEST TIME: Bridges to keep your feet dry June to September. Otherwise, any time the creek is not flooding.

WARNINGS: Wet stream crossings in winter and spring.

DIRECTIONS TO TRAILHEAD: Turn west off Highway 101 at M.123.80 onto unpaved, steep and winding Davison Road (no trailers). Go 8 miles to the Fern Canyon parking area at road's end.

FEES: $3 day use/parking ($2 for seniors).

FURTHER INFO: Prairie Creek Redwoods State Park (707) 488-2171.

*legged frog. The American dipper, or water ouzel, is a bird
that hunts insects in the stream. It actually flies under water
to catch its prey. Winter wrens are the only other birds living
in the canyon, though others may visit, like the majestic
great blue heron. Mink, river otter, coastal cutthroat and
steelhead trout round out the community.*

*The loop trail that leads through Fern Canyon is less than
¾ mile long. It has temporary bridges from June through
September. If you visit during other times of the year, you
may get your feet wet, but you will not have to contend with
the crowds of summer. Fern Canyon provides a rewarding
short walk during any season.*

Your trail begins at the Fern Canyon picnic area at the end of
the Beach Road. You head north, crossing Home Creek in
150 feet. Then your trail veers right, into the mouth of the
steep-walled canyon. You cross Home Creek twice more in
the first ⅛ mile. Take your time and observe the lush riparian
community of plants thriving here.

After ⅛ mile the steep canyon walls get higher. The north
wall rises vertically for over 60 feet at one point. Five-finger
ferns grow nearly everywhere on the sheer walls. The trail
passes under a large fallen log, which is also covered with
ferns, moss and lichens. Piggyback plants grow along the
canyon floor. The canyon winds as you cross the stream
several more times.

The canyon broadens at ¼ mile. A side trail branches right, climbing a narrow side canyon to its boxed end where a small waterfall tumbles down in winter and spring.

The main trail continues up Fern Canyon for 250 feet beyond the side trail. There a sign proclaims the end of Fern Canyon. The loop trail climbs the canyon's north wall. You ascend by uneven steps, switchbacking out of the canyon and into Sitka spruce forest. Meet the James Irvine Trail at ⅜ mile. Go left to return to the end of the Beach Road. You cross a small bridge and head northwest above the edge of the Alexander Lincoln Prairie, the site of the mining town of Gold Bluffs.

You cross a long boardwalk, then descend many steps through alder forest to return to the mouth of Fern Canyon. Energetic hikers will find many other trails in the area.

15.

BEACH/BUTLER CREEK
BOAT CREEK LOOP

WILDERNESS BEACH AND FOREST

This loop provides a marvelously varied day hike. In less than 8 miles you encounter expansive wilderness beach, a herd of wild elk, cliffs with waterfalls, steep-walled canyons, virgin forests and high ridges.

The Beach Trail heads north from road's end, paralleling the high bluffs on your right and the shore on your left. After crossing Home Creek at the mouth of Fern Canyon, you leave the alder forest for grasslands.

Less than ¼ mile from the trailhead, the Boat Creek Trail branches right and heads into the heavily wooded canyon. The Beach Trail continues along the open prairie near the beach, soon branching into two paths, one at the base of the steep bluffs, the other through open grasslands. This description stays right, but you may follow either. Keep in mind that elk live here; you may have to change trails to stay out of their way.

Your ½-mile point is marked by sandstone rocks on both sides of the trail. As you follow the edge of the forest, the surf echoes loudly from the bare cliff face above you. About ¾ mile the two paths converge briefly, then split again. Branches of spruce trees form a dense thicket on your right; elk sometimes cluster under the trees.

Before 1¼ miles a short side trail on the right leads to Gold Dust Falls, where a small stream drops 100 feet to disappear

BEACH/BUTLER CREEK/BOAT CREEK LOOP:

DISTANCE: 7¼ mile loop.

TIME: 4 hours or more.

TERRAIN: Along the beach below coastal bluffs, up a creek canyon to the ridge, then down another canyon to return to beach.

ELEVATION GAIN/LOSS: 1080 feet+/1080 feet-

BEST TIME: Spring. Fall also nice.

WARNINGS: Do not approach the elk. Give them plenty of room.

DIRECTIONS TO TRAILHEAD: Turn west off Highway 101 at M.123.8 onto unpaved, steep and winding Davison Road (no trailers). Go 8 miles to Fern Canyon parking area at end of road.

FEES: $3 day use/parking ($2 for seniors).

FURTHER INFO: Prairie Creek Redwoods State Park (707) 488-2171.

in the sandy soil beneath the spruce forest. A second waterfall is 300 feet beyond.

At 1½ miles two large slides have blocked the right path. You must veer toward the beach, but you can soon rejoin the upper path. Beyond 1¾ miles the trail veers left around some alders and passes a gravelly slide.

Approaching 2 miles you top a small rise, drop back to beach level and pass a large Sitka spruce snag. You are nearing a wedge of the forest that extends out toward the tide line, marking the mouth of Butler Creek. You enter the forest at 2¼ miles and quickly meet the Butler Creek Trail beside the creek. If you continue north along the beach, it is ½ mile to the Ossagon Creek Trail, 2 miles to Carruthers Cove (see Trails #8 and 9).

The Butler Creek Trail heads east, crossing the creek and climbing into the forest. About ½ mile from the junction, the main trail veers right where a side trail goes left into Butler Creek Camp (see Trail #11). In 250 feet another side path provides easy access to the creek. Water should be purified before drinking.

Just 200 feet east you cross the north fork of Butler Creek on a small bridge. Cross another bridge over the main creek and the path broadens. At 3¼ miles from the trailhead, your trail steepens as it climbs away from the creek. The trail climbs steadily for 1½ miles to a 900-foot summit. At 4½

miles you meet the West Ridge Trail. Make a sharp right and head southwest.

Your steady climb continues on this broad dirt road. You come to a big bend at 4⅞ miles, with an unobstructed view back to the mouth of Butler Creek. This is a good rest spot.

The trail descends slightly for ⅛ mile, passing the remains of an old shack. You resume your climb to 5¼ miles. Soon the Boat Creek Trail forks right, a narrow track where it leaves West Ridge Road.

You descend rapidly into Boat Creek Canyon, dropping 500 feet in the next ¾ mile. You pass a stand of young redwoods used by the elk as scratching posts. After a small uphill stretch, you pass the Butler Ridge Trail, a dead end that descends north.

Continue your descent, dropping rapidly by sharp switchbacks. Another side trail on the right descends into magnificent redwood groves. The main trail passes through virgin forest. At 6 miles you pass two rest benches on a steep stretch of trail.

The trail now follows the murmuring creek through the bottom of this virgin canyon. Towering redwoods rise from a dense understory of huckleberry, salal and ferns. The trail is nearly level, but the surrounding terrain is steep.

After passing a marshy section of trail, you climb briefly, then drop steadily until a steep, short drop brings you alongside the creek at 6½ miles, the first spot with easy access to the creek. A dense jungle of coastal vegetation covers the steep ground around you.

For the last ¾ mile, your trail meanders through the rugged canyon, never straying far from the now-rushing creek. Large roots grow across the trail; watch your footing. At 7 miles, within sight of the mouth of the canyon, you pass a final rest bench, on a steep slope overlooking the roaring creek.

A series of steps brings you to the mouth of the canyon, where a dense alder forest hides the virgin redwood forest upstream. From the junction with the Beach Trail it is ¼ mile south to the Fern Canyon parking area.

16.

SKUNK CABBAGE CREEK SECTION COASTAL TRAIL

NEW REDWOOD PARK TRAIL

This section of the Coastal Trail was completed in 1987. As this book went to press, the trail was unmarked at either end. It is not hard to locate, however, if you know where to look. Though the trail is described from the north, you may want to hike it from the south end, near Highway 101, for a dramatic approach to the spectacular coast.

Walk south from the wide turnout opposite the entrance station, following an old road. You may have to climb over driftwood logs, then hop over a small stream. The road parallels the beach to just before Major Creek. Then scramble over more driftwood to the beach.

The mouth of Major Creek is ⅞ mile from the trailhead. You continue south from there, heading toward the rocky outcrop called Mussel Point. Five miles offshore sits Redding Rock, a breeding ground for seabirds. At 1¼ miles you pass the mouth of a small seasonal creek. As you continue south, the beach narrows. Driftwood becomes scarce beyond the 1¾-mile point.

At 1⅞ miles a big slide on the bluff above the beach is your sign to start looking for the trail to Skunk Cabbage Creek. The trail lies about 250 feet beyond the big slide, after an outcrop of black rock laced with white veins. The trail had no marking at press time. You must look for seven wooden steps that lead up onto a steep, grassy slope. If you miss it, you will come to the prominent rock outcrop called Mussel Point in less than ¾ mile. (The beach disappears there. It is possible to scramble around the point only at the lowest tides. From there you can continue on the beach for about 2 miles to the mouth of Redwood Creek.)

Climb the steps onto the steep, grassy bluff. The trail zigzags by four switchbacks up the grassy slope scattered with lupines, poppies and other wildflowers. Just beyond 2 miles you enter a dwarf forest of alders and spruce. Climb through this forest by more switchbacks, with views of the beach and Redding Rock to the west. At 2¼ miles switch left

DISTANCE: 5½ miles, one way.

TIME: 3 hours, one way.

TERRAIN: Along the beach, then up and over a ridge to descend along a wooded creek.

ELEVATION GAIN/LOSS: One way: 520 feet+/440 feet-

BEST TIME: Spring or summer.

WARNINGS: Watch for rogue waves as you walk the beach.

DIRECTIONS TO TRAILHEAD: NORTH END: Turn west off Highway 101 at M.123.8 onto unpaved, steep Davison Road. Go 5 miles and park opposite entrance station.

SOUTH END: Turn west off Highway 101 at M.122.69 onto side road. Where road bends left, a dirt side road goes right. Watch for sign on gate: "No hunting. Redwood National Park." Trail starts/ends here.

FEES: Parking at Gold Bluffs Beach: $3 ($2 for seniors).

FURTHER INFO: Redwood National Park (707) 464-6101.

and climb steeply south-southeast toward a wooded saddle.

At the saddle a level spot provides fine views. Then your trail turns south. At 2⅜ miles you begin a gradual, winding descent to the headwaters of Skunk Cabbage Creek.

At 2½ miles you enter a dense forest of spruce to 3 feet in diameter. Rotting redwood stumps indicate that this area was logged long ago. Continue the winding descent, crossing several small bridges. Steps at 2¾ miles bring you nearer the creek. At 2⅞ miles you cross the creek on a sturdy bridge, then descend through beautiful, lichen-covered forest of spruce and alders.

After two small bridges over feeder creeks, you cross a sturdy bridge with handrails at 3¼ miles. At the next small bridge, a young redwood with its bark rubbed off stands beside the trail. Was this done by an elk or a bear? An immense snag is nearby. Standing dead trees provide habitat for birds and other animals of the forest.

After a gentle descent, cross back over Skunk Cabbage Creek at 3½ miles and wind away from the creek. A gentle climb brings you to two small bridges at 3⅝ miles.

After another small bridge at 3¾ miles, your trail meets a broad old road that it follows for most of the rest of the hike. The road runs mostly level through the gentle canyon. It is old enough for 2-foot-diameter alders to have grown in the roadbed. It has been washed away at nearly every place that a side stream crosses it.

At 3⅞ miles pass the first of these washouts. The trail bends right to cross a bridge, then returns to the old road. You soon pass another of these washouts. As you again pick up the road at 4 miles, the broad, swampy creek canyon lies on your left. Sitka spruce grow on the moist floor, which is too wet for redwoods. Many skunk cabbage also grow there.

Your trail continues in this manner, heading generally southeast. Mushrooms and other fungi thrive in this damp forest environment. At 4½ miles you enter an area logged in the last 10 to 20 years. After crossing two more bridges, you pass a lone giant redwood on the left of the trail. This area has excellent regeneration: young spruce, redwood and hemlock vie for space and light to recreate the forest.

The trail then descends a steep hill and bends right, heading into the Johnson Creek drainage. A portion of the virgin forest was spared here. Redwoods of 15 feet in diameter grow near the Johnson Creek crossing at 4⅞ miles.

By 5⅛ miles your trail again nears Skunk Cabbage Creek. But you soon climb away from the creek, passing a huge

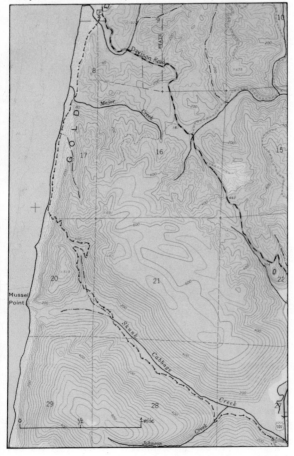

Sitka spruce. As you climb gradually to 5⅜ miles, noise from the highway begins to intrude. You have fine views of the valley where Skunk Cabbage Creek and Prairie Creek converge. You descend to the southern trailhead, a locked gate beside a paved road, 5½ miles from your starting point.

17.

LOST MAN CREEK
OLD ROAD THROUGH VIRGIN FOREST TO VIEWS

One of the least used trails in Redwood National Park, Lost Man Creek Trail lies 2 miles east of Highway 101 on a gravel road. It provides easy access to a beautiful redwood grove beside the pristine pools and rapids of the creek. Photographers love its combination of forest, clearings and creek. People in wheelchairs can reach the picnic area, restrooms and first portion of trail.

In 1982 a special dedication ceremony took place here. Redwood National Park was designated a World Heritage Site by UNESCO, the United Nations Educational, Scientific and Cultural Organization. About 200 international sites have been chosen as World Heritage Sites because of natural and cultural properties of outstanding universal value to the human race.

The short, easy ramble becomes a more arduous hike if you continue beyond the third bridge. The trail steepens and soon enters lands that were logged. You can continue for up to 10 miles, where you reach Bald Hills Road, about a mile north of C-Line Road.

The parking area is a clearing beside Lost Man Creek. You pass through a stile (broad enough for wheelchairs) and immediately come to several picnic tables in a pleasantly shaded spot above the creek. Head southeast on the graveled Geneva Road, climbing gradually through the forest. At ¼ mile you cross a bridge over Lost Man Creek. From the bridge you have fine views of the rocky pools upstream.

Your climb steepens after the bridge. You recross the creek in 200 feet. The trail continues to climb moderately, the creek again on your right. The path levels briefly at ½ mile, then climbs gently. The forest here is mixed in size and species. Redwoods and Douglas firs range from small to

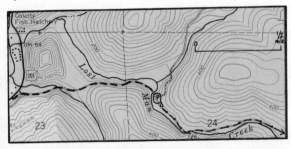

LOST MAN CREEK:

DISTANCE: 2 miles, round trip.
   10 miles, one way to Bald Hills Road.
TIME: One hour or all day.
TERRAIN: Through picturesque virgin forest alongside creek, then climb old roads through logged area to high ridge.
ELEVATION GAIN/LOSS: 1st mile: 160 feet+/-, round trip.
   To Holter Ridge:1340 feet+/1340 feet-, round trip.
   To Bald Hills Road: 2400 feet+/520 feet-, one way.

BEST TIME: Anytime.
WARNINGS: Bicycles not allowed. Very steep after the first 1½ miles.
DIRECTIONS TO TRAILHEAD: Turn east off Highway 101 at M.124.4 and follow gravel road 1.9 miles to picnic area at its end.
FURTHER INFO: Redwood National Park (707) 464-6101.

giant. An understory of redwood-associated plants includes sword and deer ferns, salal, redwood sorrel, and salmon-, thimble- and huckleberry.

At ¾ mile your trail levels again, drawing alongside the creek. Then you climb gradually again as you angle away from the creek. You come to a logged area at one mile. Here you cross a creek that enters Lost Man Creek from the north.

Then the old road begins to climb a long, steep hill, with views of the cascading creek on your right. You re-enter virgin forest as you begin to climb high above the creek. Those preferring an easy hike should turn back before climbing far up the hill. By 1½ miles you are 100 feet above Lost Man Creek. Below to the south the creek splits. The main fork flows down from far to the south. Geneva Road climbs steeply up a side drainage coming from the east.

The road steepens at 1½ miles. After 1¾ miles the forest starts to thin as the habitat becomes drier. You turn briefly north before 2 miles, where the road almost levels, providing relief from the steady climb. The climb steepens again as you turn east, then northeast. After 2¼ miles the forest has been logged. You have occasional views down to the virgin forest of Lost Man Creek.

By 2½ miles you have climbed 1000 feet from the trailhead. The road continues to climb without relief until you level at 3¾ miles and come to a fork in the road. You are on the eastern park boundary at a 1500-foot elevation. To continue, turn right onto Holter Ridge Road. It generally follows the ridge and the park boundary south to meet Bald Hills Road in about 6 more miles, climbing to an elevation of 2300 feet. You meet Bald Hills Road in its sixth mile.

18.

LADY BIRD JOHNSON GROVE LOOP

LUSH HIGHLAND VIRGIN FOREST

When she was First Lady, Lady Bird Johnson spoke out for the creation of Redwood National Park. Her stand helped break a deadlock in Congress over establishment of the controversial park, and the acquisition funds were allocated. Appropriately, she came to dedicate the park in 1968. The ceremony occurred in what is today called Lady Bird Johnson Grove.

A short, easy loop trail, 1⅜ miles in length, explores the virgin grove, located on a high ridge. People in wheelchairs can follow the trail with little or no assistance.

The master plan for trail development in Redwood National Park includes plans for a trail to connect the coast

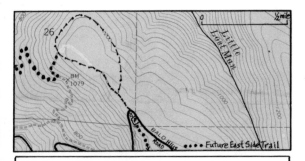

LADY BIRD JOHNSON GROVE LOOP:

DISTANCE: 1⅜-mile loop.

TIME: 30 to 60 minutes.

TERRAIN: High ridge between Redwood Creek and Little Lost Man Creek.

ELEVATION GAIN/LOSS: 150 feet+/150 feet-

BEST TIME: Spring for wildflowers.

WARNINGS: Steep winding road to trailhead not advisable for trailers.

DIRECTIONS TO TRAILHEAD: Turn east off Highway 101 at M.122.0 onto Bald HIlls Road. Go 2.6 miles to the Lady Bird Johnson parking area on the right.

FURTHER INFO: Redwood National Park (707) 464-6101.

with the east side of the Redwood Creek basin. One segment of the trail would head south from the LBJ Grove parking area. Another section, 3¼ miles in length, would descend from the north end of the Grove Loop to meet Bald Hills Road near Highway 101. The trails will not be finished before the late 1990s.

The trail leaves the parking area and crosses Bald Hills Road on a pedestrian bridge. In 200 feet a dispenser provides pamphlets for the self-guiding nature trail. The trail heads northwest through virgin forest of redwood, Douglas fir, grand fir and hemlock. This high-elevation forest differs from the coastal forests of redwood and Sitka spruce and the drier forests farther inland.

The trail climbs gently along the north end of Bald Hills Ridge. Numerous rest benches provide stopping places. The lush understory growth is dominated by salal, sword fern, red and evergreen huckleberry, salmonberry and red-flowering currant. Other understory plants include tanoak, wild rose, redwood sorrel, coltsfoot, redwood violet, rhododendron and blue flag iris.

At ¼ mile a rest bench sits at the spot where the return trail enters on the right. The trail levels, then starts a gradual descent. Salmonberries grow to 10 feet tall here.

The easy descent continues to ½ mile, where a plaque on the right marks the spot of the 1968 dedication of Redwood National Park by Lady Bird Johnson. The redwoods here have broad, thick-barked trunks but do not grow as tall as the trees sheltered in the deep, protected canyons. The maximum heights are generally less than 250 feet.

Soon the Pacific Ocean peeks through the trees as you near the edge of a clearcut. Most of the land between here and the coast is now protected in state and national parks. The trail bends right at the edge of the clearcut, then starts a gentle climb. You encounter the hollylike leaves of Oregon grape.

About ¾ mile from the trailhead, your trail bends right again and heads southeast. On your left the forest drops steeply toward Little Lost Man Creek, ½ mile away and 700 feet below. Your trail levels before ⅞ mile. Giant rhododendrons grow on the left with trunks 4 inches in diameter.

The level path continues through a forest of big trees with a lush understory. In spring trilliums and redwood sorrel present white and purple flowers. Tiny calypso and coral root orchids may also grow along the trail. Licorice ferns grow on the bark of trees. Native Americans mixed them with the tobacco they grew to sweeten the smoke.

At one mile a rest bench sits beside the edge of the steep drop into Little Lost Man Creek. The trail climbs a short hill, then descends gradually to meet the return trail at 1⅛ miles. Turn left and descend ¼ mile to the parking area.

19.

REDWOOD CREEK

EASY BACKPACK TO TALL TREES

Two trails reach the Tall Trees Grove of Redwood National Park. Both routes have seasonal limitations; hikers must heed the warnings about off-season travel on both the Redwood Creek and Tall Trees Trails. To ignore them could mean disaster at the worst, or a ruined trip or cold night in the woods, at the least. Redwood Creek Trail is the longer route into Tall Trees Grove. This easy trek avoids the steep

REDWOOD CREEK:

DISTANCE: 8½ miles, one way. 17 miles, round trip.

TIME: 4-5 hours, one way.

TERRAIN: Follows the wandering, nearly level canyon of Redwood Creek.

ELEVATION GAIN/LOSS: One way: 420 feet+/390 feet- Round trip: 810 feet+/810 feet-

BEST TIME: Late spring or fall for solitude. May 15 to September 15 for bridges.

WARNINGS: Creek fords are usually treacherous to impassable during rainy season (October-April); inquire before you go. Watch for poison oak.

DIRECTIONS TO TRAILHEAD: Turn east off Highway 101 at M.122.0 onto Bald Hills Road. Go .4 mile to parking area on right.

FURTHER INFO: Redwood National Park (707) 464-6101.

OTHER SUGGESTION: A HORSE TRAIL leaves from the Orick Rodeo grounds on Bald Hills Road, just east of Highway 101. About 27 miles of trail loop through clearcut areas and some old growth forest west of Redwood Creek.

CROSS COUNTRY HIKING: In summer the most rewarding backcountry experience comes to the hiker who walks the gravel bars of Redwood Creek. The creek repeatedly swings across the route, forcing the hiker to ford knee-deep water. You can go about 14 miles before the steep, narrow gorge of Rocky Gap bars progress. You can camp anywhere on the gravel bars, except within ¼ mile of the Tall Trees crossing.

terrain surrounding Redwood Creek by following the creek's gradual canyon upstream. The problem for off-season travelers lies in the two crossings of the creek. In summer (generally May to September; inquire at Redwood Information Center) temporary bridges are installed at the crossings. In late spring and early fall, when the bridges have been removed, you can usually ford the creek (inquire!) to find solitude at Tall Trees Grove. But as waters rise with the rains, you cannot get beyond the first ford.

From the parking area, the Redwood Creek Trail heads southeast. The level trail passes through a streamside forest of alders, bay laurels and willows. You pass your first redwood after ⅛ mile. The young tree on the right is dwarfed by a huge old redwood stump with spring board cuts on the left.

These notches indicate that this area was logged long ago, before the advent of chain saws.

Your trail soon comes to the bank of Redwood Creek. From here you have your most expansive view up the creek, with big redwoods along both sides. In 100 feet you come to a station where you can write your own backcountry camping and fire permit.

You continue southeast beyond ¼ mile, where you cross a bridge over a side stream, then turn south. At ½ mile you come to a big meadow between the trail and Redwood Creek. Blackberries thrive in the sunny clearing.

You come to a second meadow at ⅝ mile. Your trail bends right and brings you alongside the creek again at ¾ mile. An osprey nest sits atop a tall tree about 200 feet east of the meadow. You continue across two small bridges into an area of lush riparian vegetation. Sitka spruce, alder, salmonberry, water hemlock and piggyback plant grow here.

You pass through a third meadow at 1⅛ miles, right beside the gravel bed of the creek. A riot of wildflowers grows here in the spring. After the meadow comes an immense berry patch, then an area where stinging nettles crowd the trail in late spring and summer. The next meadow stretches along the trail for ¼ mile. At its end you come to a tunnel of vegetation, then drop onto the gravel bar of the creekbed. You are 1½ miles from the trailhead.

In summer you cross the creek on a temporary bridge. But in the off-season you must ford the creek. The gravel crossing 200 feet upstream from where the trail meets the creek usually provides the best ford. To find the trail south, look for the two red diamonds on the opposite bank, south-southwest from where you meet the creek. When the author hiked here in October, two mergansers floated downstream, perturbed by my intrusion

On the west bank duck under a fallen maple and enter more riparian forest. On your right a giant maple stands against a fern-covered cliff. After 1¾ miles drop to a crossing of McArthur Creek. Your trail then runs along the base of the steep canyon wall until you descend onto the gravel bed of Redwood Creek at 2 miles. On the canyon wall grow five-finger and sword ferns and many piggyback plants. Bracken and deer ferns grow a bit farther along the trail. At 2¼ miles pass a large redwood on your left, then climb a short, steep hill. This is followed by three short up and down stretches.

You drop to a bridge over Elam Creek at 2⅝ miles. The canyon becomes very broad here. Cross a small seasonal creek and head due east at 2⅞ miles, passing under large maples draped with lichen.

Your level trail stays near Redwood Creek, making a big,

slow bend to the right. Drop back beside the creek at 3½ miles, heading south. Pass some big redwoods before the trail veers onto the gravel bar of Redwood Creek at 3⅝ miles.

You are soon back under the alders. At 3¾ miles the steep slope of the canyon is right by the trail. The trail passes under a huge, still-growing fallen redwood. After crossing a small stream, you come to a broad spot in the trail at 4 miles, a pleasant rest spot with dry ground and a good view of Redwood Creek Canyon.

The trail continues upstream, mostly level by the creek. After 4¼ miles you enter a logged area. Only a few small- to medium-sized redwoods remain. Make a gradual climb to 4½ miles, then cross a bridge high over an unnamed creek. Cross two more bridges over nameless creeks in the next ¼ mile, then descend alongside Redwood Creek again at 5 miles.

After large redwood stumps at 5¼ miles, you start another gradual climb. By 5½ miles you are about 100 feet above big pools in Redwood Creek. You drop quickly to a bridge over Bond Creek, then angle left at 5¾ miles and climb gradually, heading southeast. This is the biggest climb on your way to Tall Trees Grove; you gain 200 feet in the next ¾ mile. You pass a stand of virgin redwoods but most of the remainder of the trail passes through an area clearcut before this became a national park. A young alder forest has grown quickly to cover the scars and provide shade along most of your route. The shade of alders also helps the light-sensitive young redwoods get established.

A wooden post marks the 6-mile point of your hike. You continue to climb, passing another stand of virgin redwoods below the trail. You come to a sunny rest bench at the top of the hill. Then you descend gradually to cross a rustic bridge over cascading Fortyfour Creek.

Begin another gradual ascent, gaining 100 feet in a mile to reach the highest elevation on the trail, 290 feet above sea level, at 7⅜ miles. Your broad trail follows what was once a major logging road. Ruffed grouse nest along this section of the trail. One might spook with a noisy flurry of wings.

The road narrows and levels as you come to a sign marking the 7½-mile point. You arrive at the top of a large slide stretching 180 feet down to Redwood Creek. Next to a wooden guardrail you have a fine view of Tall Trees Grove to your southeast and Redwood Creek snaking through the canyon below. This is one of the best places in the redwood country to see the immense size these ancient trees can attain. The creek looks so far below you, yet the tops of the gargantuan redwoods rise far above you. Can you tell which one is the world's tallest tree? (Hint: it has one live top and

one dead top.)

For the next ⅝ mile your trail descends, circling the Tall Trees Grove. You can see the grove through breaks in the alder forest as you descend along a cool north slope. Young redwoods grow on the right of the trail.

You reach the bottom of the hill and a trail register at 8⅛ miles. Sign in here, like fellow visitors from around the world. A sign indicates that camping is not allowed within .3 mile of the Tall Trees crossing. Pause here once more to appreciate the heights of the trees across the creek. Once you are in the grove you will be too close to get any sense of their height.

It is 500 feet across the creek and into the grove. A temporary footbridge crosses the creek from May to September. In other months you will have to get your feet wet. When you reach the grove, the tallest tree is on your left. A ⅝ mile loop trail circles through the Tall Trees Grove. It passes under immense big leaf maples, then leads to the third and sixth tallest trees. It also passes a brine vat used by an early settler to salt the fish he caught in the creek.

If you are camping on Redwood Creek, put on your old tennis shoes and shorts and hike upstream along the gravel bars. As the creek wanders from one side of the canyon to the other, you must ford the azure stream many times. But you are rewarded with solitude, as well as a chance to sight herons, ducks, hawks, perhaps even a golden eagle, black bear, mountain lion or fox. Or perhaps you can spot their tracks in sand along the creek.

It is 1½ miles upstream to the Emerald Ridge Trail (see Trail #20). You can continue about two more miles before you encounter Rocky Gap, a narrow, steep-walled jumble of huge boulders that blocks further progress. Only hikers with rock climbing experience and a minimum party size of three should attempt to get beyond Rocky Gap.

If you camp on the gravel bars of Redwood Creek, treat your drinking water, hang food from bears, bury body waste at least 150 feet from the water, do not wash or let even biodegradable soap get into the streams, and use only dead, downed wood for fires. Of course hikers should carry out all their trash at all times.

20.

TALL TREES
EMERALD RIDGE LOOP
EASY WAY IN TO REDWOODS, STEEP WALK OUT

From late May until the end of summer, a shuttle bus runs from the Redwood Information Center south of Orick to the Tall Trees Trailhead. The bus leaves about every 1½ hours, stopping at the Redwood Creek Trailhead along the way. When the bus is running, it provides the easy way to the Tall Trees Grove, making it accessible to day hikers. You may also bring a backpack on the shuttle, camp along Redwood Creek, then hike out on the Redwood Creek Trail (see Trail #19) for the full tour.

When the bus is not running, you may park on Bald Hills Road opposite the C-Line Road. You can then hike down to the Tall Trees. (The road is closed to bikes and motorized traffic other than the shuttle bus.) The unpaved gravel road descends about 1000 feet in 6 miles to reach Tall Trees Trailhead. The hike in is easy, but the hike out is a grunt. If you take this route to Tall Trees Grove in winter, you will not be able to cross swift-flowing Redwood Creek when you get there, requiring that you return the way you went in.

After passing through the clearcuts along C-Line Road for 5.9 miles, you come to the bus stop shelter beside the Tall Trees Trail. The trail descends south, quickly passing two shady picnic spots with tables. The ridge to the west of the trail was saved from logging, making this a pleasantly

TALL TREES/EMERALD RIDGE LOOP:

DISTANCE: 1¼ miles, one way. 2½ miles, round trip. 4 mile loop. Also off-season hike access: 5.9 miles one way to trailhead.

TIME: To Tall Trees: 30 minutes. Return to bus stop: 45 minutes to an hour. Emerald Loop: 2 to 3 hours.

TERRAIN: Descend steeply to the world's tallest trees in a big bend of Redwood Creek.

ELEVATION GAIN/LOSS: From shuttle bus stop: 500 feet-To Tall Trees Grove, 500 feet+ to return
From Bald Hills Road: 1500 feet-/1500 feet+, round trip

BEST TIME: Shuttle bus runs May to September. Off season, the long hike provides solitude and serenity.

WARNINGS: Redwood Creek cannot be forded in winter. Steep trail on return hike. Watch for poison oak.

DIRECTIONS TO TRAILHEAD: Turn east off Highway 101 onto Bald Hills Road at M.122.0. Go 7.1 miles to Tall Trees parking area on left. Or take the shuttle bus from Redwood Information Center.

FEES: Shuttle bus: $3 adults, $1 child (15 and under), $1.50 62 and over or permanently disabled.

FURTHER INFO: Redwood National Park (707) 464-6101.

shaded hike. A forest of redwoods and Douglas firs to 4 feet in diameter provides shade for you and the lush understory plants: rhododendrons, huckleberries, ceanothus, salal, chinquapins and tanoaks. These are soon joined by western hemlocks and lichen-draped maples, and an occasional Port Orford cedar.

At ⅛ mile you come to a junction; the Emerald Ridge Trail on the left heads southeast, while the main trail turns west. Descending toward the grove, the habitat grows more moist and the trees are larger. Rest benches sit along the trail.

You turn northwest after ¼ mile and draw closer to the ridge. The trail zigzags, descending to where a small stream cascades down the steep hillside. Cross another small creek at ⅝ mile, where deer and sword ferns thrive. You continue to descend, passing more rest benches.

Your trail levels at an older alluvial flat deposited by Redwood Creek eons ago, before it had cut as deep a canyon as it follows today. At one mile a sign indicates "Tall Trees Grove." A redwood with a goose pen stands on the right. You descend once again, coming to restrooms at 1⅛ miles. Then you drop quickly to the floor of Tall Trees Grove, meeting the

Redwood Creek Trail (see Trail #19) at 1¼ miles. Go right for 250 feet to meet the world's tallest tree. The twin trunks of the 600-year-old Tall Tree rise 367.8 feet, the trunk on the right being the tallest. Also in this grove are the third tallest (364.3 feet), fifth and sixth tallest trees.

Be sure to take time to walk the ⅜-mile loop trail that winds through the grove. If you want a longer hike but do not want to hike 8.2 miles on the Redwood Creek Trail, you can make the Emerald Ridge Loop described below.

You can only hike upstream along Redwood Creek during the time of low water, generally from May until October. Even then you must make several knee-deep crossings of the creek. Head upstream from the Redwood Creek Trail crossing, just south of Tall Trees Grove. You head east for ½ mile. Then the creek and canyon make a big bend right. You turn south about ¾ mile, then head south-southeast as the creek bed broadens to wide gravel bars. An old road meets the west side of Redwood Creek just after one mile. The creek bends left until you are heading southeast. About 1¼ miles, creek and canyon bend farther to the left.

Soon a stream with a small waterfall enters Redwood Creek on your right, by some lichen-covered rocks. A pleasant swimming hole is here in summer. The Emerald Ridge Trail is about 200 feet beyond. It heads north from the southernmost bend in this section of Redwood Creek. If you fail to notice the trail, you will come to Emerald Creek on your left within ¼ mile. *IF YOU COME TO EMERALD CREEK YOU HAVE PASSED THE TRAIL.* (You can follow Redwood Creek for 2 miles to Rocky Gap, where you can go no farther.)

The Emerald Ridge Trail climbs away from Redwood Creek, passing a huge circle of redwoods on the right. As you climb through forest with 8-foot diameter redwoods, you can glimpse the canyon of Emerald Creek below.

At 2 miles from the Tall Trees Grove, you climb away from the creek, and the habitat becomes drier. The trail heads generally northwest. You descend briefly just before 2¼ miles. A redwood root ball of fine geometric shape lies on the left. You climb gradually again before leveling amidst many large rhododendrons. Then resume your climb, winding around a shattered and scarred redwood giant.

You gain the crest of Emerald Ridge at 2½ miles and wind along it, climbing steeply, then more gradually. You climb northeast with several switchbacks through a forest of fire-scarred redwoods, scattered hemlocks and Douglas firs. The trail climbs and winds through the forest, leaving the ridge and heading north after 2⅝ miles. Then you turn west and climb more steeply. After two more turns you meet the Tall

Trees Trail ⅛ mile from the shuttle bus stop. Turn right and climb back to the trailhead. The entire loop is 4 miles, 4⅜ miles with the loop through Tall Trees Grove.

21.

DRY LAGOON TO
BIG LAGOON BEACH

BARRIER BEACH ALONG LAGOON SHORE

In 1931 the Department of Parks and Recreation acquired the Gillis Ranch and made it a state park. Today Humboldt Lagoons State Park encompasses 1036 acres. The hike along the barrier beach of Big Lagoon has a wilderness feeling. In winter or at extreme high tides, it may be impassable as high water breaches the barrier. When the author hiked here in spring 1988, the beach was impassable at a tide of +4.0 feet or more. But this figure varies from one season to another. If you arrive at high tide, you can picnic at the tables surrounding the parking area while you wait for the tide to recede.

A pleasant walk-in or bike-in campground lies south and east of the trailhead and picnic area. Six beautiful sites are located in a spruce forest, some with views of the ocean or Dry Lagoon. The camps have tables, fire pits, food cabinets and pit toilets, but you must bring your own water. They cost $6 per night.

The second most populous Yurok village on the coast was Opyuweg or Oketo (meaning lake), located at the southwest corner of Big Lagoon. Four smaller villages were on the eastern shore. The Yuroks would take their redwood dugout canoes out onto the 1470-acre lagoon to fish.

Prospectors came through here after the 1849 gold strikes on the Klamath and Trinity Rivers. Following the Gold Bluffs excitement, some prospectors worked Big Lagoon's barrier beach in the 1850s, but with little success. Ranchers settled the area in the 1870s. Timber firms acquired the forests to the east about the same time, although no logging occurred here until after World War II.

In the 1990s the Coastal Trail will lead north from here to Stone Lagoon. It will wind east to an Environmental Camp on the south shore of Stone Lagoon, then follow the shore to the existing drive-in campground.

To get to the barrier beach of Big Lagoon, go left from the parking area and follow the beach, which runs south-southwest from here. The high, wooded bluff on your left is the site of the Dry Lagoon Environmental Camps.

Walking the beach of salt-and-pepper pebbly sand, you come to the first of several large rocks at tide line after ⅛ mile. At ¼ mile a landslide on the bluff has made the beach very narrow at high tide. Consult your tide table before proceeding. If the tide is higher than +4.0 feet for your hike, you may not be able to pass this point on your return. While the bluff has slide activity for the next ⅜ mile, the narrowest point was at the ¼-mile point as of this writing.

More rocks are scattered along the tide line, including a very large one at ⅜ mile. If the surf is large on the day of your hike, watch out for waves that surge through the gaps in the shoreline rocks. After ⅜ mile the beach broadens. After the

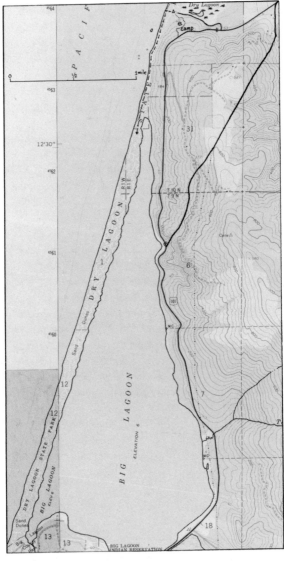

DRY LAGOON TO BIG LAGOON BEACH:

DISTANCE: Round trip as described: 6 miles (can go 8½ miles or more).

TIME: 2-4 hours.

TERRAIN: Barrier beach between ocean and Big Lagoon.

BEST TIME: Medium to low tide.

WARNINGS: Beach may be impassable at high tide of +4 feet or more. In winter, the lagoon breaches its barrier and the beach walk may be impassable. Do not get cut off by the rising tide. Watch for rogue waves as you walk on the beach.

DIRECTIONS TO TRAILHEAD: NORTH END: Turn west off Highway 101 at M.114.3. Go 1.0 miles to end of road and beach parking area.

SOUTH END: Turn west off Highway 101 at M.108.4 onto Roundhouse Creek Road. Go .3 mile, then turn right on Big Lagoon Park Road. Go .5 mile to day use parking area.

FEES: NORTH END: None. SOUTH END: $2.00

FURTHER INFO: Information and reservations for environmental camps: (707) 488-2171

Big Lagoon County Park: (707) 445-7652

OTHER SUGGESTION: At STONE LAGOON, a similar hike leads along the lagoon's shore, for a hike of 2 to 3½ miles. The final ¾ mile to Sharp Point may be inaccessible at high tide. The trail leaves from the southwest corner of the campground. At DRY LAGOON, a one-mile loop trail leads through the Environmental Camps and follows a portion of old highway. From Dry Lagoon Beach parking area, you can also walk the BEACH NORTH to Sharp Point, less than one mile.

SOUTH END: You can also walk Big Lagoon's barrier beach north from Big Lagoon County Park. See directions to trailhead.

landslide at ⅝ mile, you can see Big Lagoon ahead.

You reach the north end of the lagoon at ¾ mile. At the flood channel here, Big Lagoon may drain into the Pacific after breaching. At extreme high tides, waves may dump their salt water into the lagoon here as well. If you can cross the flood channel, you climb to the high barrier beach beyond. At ⅞ mile a driftwood log rests atop the barrier beach, providing a bench overlooking lagoon and channel. Big Lagoon stretches south for more than 3 miles.

Walk the crest of the barrier beach, heading toward Patrick's Point. At one mile you encounter scattered pockets of coastal strand vegetation; yellow-flowered northern dune tansy and sand verbena dominate.

The barrier beach broadens at 1⅛ miles and stays very broad for ½ mile. Low dunes provide shelter for salt-tolerant plants. Sea rocket and sea fig join the dune tansy and sand verbena. Denser vegetation grows along the lagoon's shore. Big Lagoon is an important stop on the Pacific Flyway. Thousands of birds rest and feed here in the winter. Year-round residents include members of the heron family, egrets and various shore birds.

After 1⅝ miles the barrier beach gradually narrows as Big Lagoon increases in width. Dense patches of dune and cord grass grow near the lagoon's shore, providing nesting cover for shore birds. At 2⅛ miles, you come to the first of several low spots in the beach. At extremely high tides, the breakers carry over the top of the sand spit, adding sea water to the brackish waters of the lagoon. About 30 species of fish inhabit the lagoon, as well as Dungeness crab, soft-shelled clams and bay mussels.

Continuing along the crest of the barrier beach, you encounter beach strawberry and seaside daisy growing with the other coastal-strand plants. Two more high-tide breaches lie at 2½ miles. The sand along the crest gets softer and looser here. You might want to veer west to the hard-packed sand near tide line. If you do, watch out for the large, churning waves that break quickly and run up the beach. An extremely violent undertow lies offshore as well. You can also veer east to the lagoon's shore.

At 2⅞ miles a log atop the beach crest is posted "State Park Property." At 3 miles Big Lagoon is over a mile across. Highway 101 runs along the east shore. A dense forest of windblown redwood, Sitka spruce and grand fir grows there. On the barrier beach, large driftwood logs provide seating and some shelter for a picnic and/or birdwatching.

It is 1¼ miles farther to Big Lagoon County Park on the south shore. Beach-walk fanatics can continue another 2 miles along Agate Beach to Patrick's Point State Park.

Most hikers will want to turn back by the 3-mile point, for a 6-mile round trip. Before you do, notice the spectacular view of the rugged coastline of Agate Beach and Patrick's Point. You may want to walk closer to the lagoon's shore on your return, watching for birds as you go. But try to stay above the dense patches of grass along the shore so as not to disturb the birds and other small native creatures living there. Plan 1½ hours for your return.

PATRICK'S POINT STATE PARK

This 632-acre state park sits upon a level promontory surrounded on three sides by the rugged Pacific Ocean. Long ago the level headland was beneath the Pacific before sea level receded. Ceremonial Rock and Lookout Rock now stand high above the headland. When the headland was flooded they were sea stacks, like the ones offshore today.

The park was named for Patrick Beegan who homesteaded the area in 1851. Patrick's Point became a state park in 1929. The seasonal Yurok village of Sumig was at Patrick's Point.

The annual rainfall averages 65 inches, most of it falling between October and April. Coastal fog can shroud the headland almost year-round. It occasionally lingers for days at a time, especially in summer. But spring and fall often bring crystal-clear days, making those seasons the best time to visit. On the clearest days you can stand atop Ceremonial Rock and see the mouth of the Klamath River, 30 miles north. From the top of Wedding Rock you may be able to see Cape Mendocino, 50 miles south.

22.

AGATE BEACH
CLIFFS ABOVE THE CRESCENT SHORE

From the northeast corner of the parking lot, you head northeast, then east, descending 24 steps to the best view of Agate Beach, 160 feet below. Beyond the beach lie Big Lagoon and Sharp Point. Descend more steps through Sitka spruce forest. Understory plants include dense salal up to 5 feet thick, coltsfoot, azalea and yellow skunk cabbage.

At ⅛ mile a picnic table on the right has a fine view of Agate Beach. Then your trail descends north along a narrow ridge between two ravines. The forest gives way to dense coastal scrub of salal, bush lupine, coastal manroot, yarrow, elderberry, blackberry and red-flowering currant.

As you descend toward the beach, you have an excellent view of the evenly tilted sandstone strata in the cliff above the beach. Your trail bends to the left and descends steeply to the beach at ¼ mile.

The beach ends at a cliff 300 feet west of the trail. It

AGATE BEACH:

DISTANCE: ½ mile round trip to beach, up to 4½ miles round trip.

TIME: 30 minutes or more.

TERRAIN: Quick, steep descent to beach backed by high cliffs. Don't forget the steep climb back to trailhead.

ELEVATION GAIN/LOSS: 180 feet+/180 feet-

BEST TIME: Spring for wildflowers. Low tide for greatest beach access. After winter storms for agate and jade collecting.

WARNINGS: Dangerous undertow here. It is unsafe to wade or swim.

DIRECTIONS TO TRAILHEAD: Exit Highway 101 onto Patrick's Point Drive (from north at M.106.6, from south at M.106.4). Go .5 mile to park entrance, where you turn right. Go past entrance station and follow signs to Agate Beach. The parking area is one mile from the park entrance.

FEES: $3 day use. $10 camping. $2 hike/bike camping.

FURTHER INFO: Patrick's Point State Park (707) 677-3570.

OTHER SUGGESTION: OCTOPUS TREES NATURE TRAIL leaves .1 mile beyond Agate Beach Trailhead, looping through a grove of Sitka spruce. The ¼-mile trail features the park's plant life.

CEREMONIAL ROCK is reached by several trails of about ¼ mile in length. You climb 94 steps to the top of the 287-foot-high ancient sea stack. It was used for ceremonies by the Yuroks.

extends northeast, then north for 7 miles. It is 2 miles to the south end of Big Lagoon. The broad beach then continues north to Sharp Point.

From the stairway, walk northeast for 75 feet to cross a small creek. The mouth of the creek has layers of dark graywacke sandstone, backed by towering cliffs of light yellow sandstone (unfortunately defaced by carvings of names and initials). Continuing along the beach, at ⅜ mile you are beyond the steepest portion of the sandstone cliff. The beach curves north in a gentle crescent.

At ½ mile lupine covers the face of the cliff, providing a

spectacular display of color at the peak of bloom from April to June. At ¾ mile a steep gully cuts through the cliff. Just beyond the gully, the magnificent cliffs reach their highest point, rising almost vertically for 400 feet.

By now you may have seen people scurrying along the beach with collecting bags. Rockhounds frequent Agate Beach to collect small pieces of agate and black jade polished by the waves and cast upon the beach.

Continue along the beach as long as you wish, leaving time to return to the trailhead before sunset. Beyond the one-mile point, you will have improving views back to the spectacular, rocky coastline of Patrick's Point.

After your return walk along the beach, you end your hike by climbing 247 steps to the trailhead.

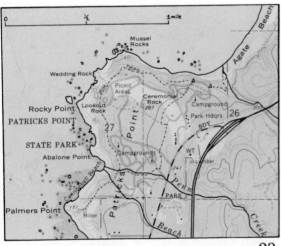

23.

RIM LOOP

STAIRS, SEA STACKS AND BEACHES

The Rim Trail follows an old Yurok path along the edge of the park headlands. This easy, mostly level trail provides access to six steep spur trails that lead to promontories with breathtaking views. You can approach most of these spur trails by car, but the Rim Trail provides an intimate look at the wild side of Patrick's Point.

The trail described begins at Agate Beach Trailhead and parking area, then circles the shore in a counter-clockwise direction. It circles back through the center of the park to your starting point. The trail is 3⅛ miles long without any of the spur trails, 4½ miles long if you take them all.

Head west from the parking area, descending along an

obtrusive chain link fence. (The fence prevents foolish people from risking life and limb on the steep 200-foot bluff that drops to the ocean.) In 300 feet a wide spot provides an excellent view of Agate Beach. Sitka spruce, Bishop pine and Douglas fir rise above a dense understory of salal, berry vines, ferns and azaleas.

At ⅛ mile a spur trail meets the main trail. On your right is another fine view, with Mussel Rocks visible to the northwest and Agate Beach to the northeast. Red alders and shore pines join the forest as you continue through a small gully. Then eight-foot-tall thimbleberries shade the path.

Enter dense forest again at ¼ mile. Tiny Beaver Creek gurgles on your left. Soon you turn right toward the edge of the bluff and another overlook. The trail bends left, crossing a bridge above a waterfall. At ⅜ mile you pass through a dense tunnel of brush and descend some steps to meet the Mussel Rocks trail on your right.

If you turn right, the path descends steeply to the rocks, with a fantastic view of Agate Beach stretching north to Big Lagoon. It is ⅛ mile to the end of the spur, where you can fish or look. Climb 146 steps to return to the Rim Trail.

The Rim Trail climbs steps to the ½-mile point where your trail levels and heads south. You pass between two big rocks, then descend stone steps to a convenient picnic spot.

Your trail heads west to another view of the coast. After ⅝ mile you pass another picnic spot (with a water spigot). As you approach the Wedding Rock parking area, take the first right fork to avoid the congestion at the popular day-use area. You meet the Wedding Rock spur trail before ¾ mile.

The Wedding Rock spur descends rough steps, then climbs to reach the top of Wedding Rock at ⅛ mile. From the top of the 120-foot-high ancient sea stack, you have a spectacular view of the coast to the south. This is also a great spot for whale watching and storm watching.

Returning to the Rim Trail, head south. You climb steps to join a paved, wheelchair-accessible path, then meet the Patrick's Point spur trail.

The Patrick's Point trail branches right. The paved path descends to a picture-postcard view of Wedding Rock and the surrounding coast. The detour to Patrick's Point and back totals ¼ mile.

The Rim Trail wraps around the base of Lookout Rock on your left to meet the Lookout Rock spur in just 150 feet. (It is ⅛ mile to the top of the ancient sea stack and back.)

Then the Rim Trail descends gradually through Sitka spruce forest. Before ⅞ mile you cross tiny Ickie Ughie Creek. In 200 feet you meet the Rocky Point side trail. (Turn right to walk down to Rocky Point. It is ⅛ mile to the point

RIM LOOP:

DISTANCE: 3⅛- to 4½-mile loop.

TIME: 2-3 hours.

TERRAIN: Follow a convoluted shore through dense vegetation, with access to rocky points and beaches. Loop back through the center of the park.

ELEVATION GAIN/LOSS: Rim Loop: 180 feet+/180 feet-
To Mussel Rock, Wedding Rock and Abalone Point: add 320 feet+/320 feet-

BEST TIME: Spring and fall.

WARNINGS: Stay back from edge of steep cliffs. Watch for poison oak. On the shore, never turn your back on the ocean; watch for rogue waves.

DIRECTIONS TO TRAILHEAD: Exit Highway 101 onto Patrick's Point Drive at M.106.6 (north) or M.106.4 (south). Go .5 mile to park entrance and turn right. Follow signs to Agate Beach parking area, about one mile.

FEES: $3 day use/parking.

FURTHER INFO: Patrick's Point State Park (707) 677-3570.

and back.)

Beyond the Rocky Point spur, the Rim Trail climbs a hill to meet a trail to the hike/bike camps. Then head south through alder forest. The relatively open forest provides glimpses of the rugged coast. At one mile from the trailhead, a large cypress stands between the trail and the sea. You continue through forest and coastal scrub along the western edge of Abalone Campground. At 1⅛ miles you meet the side trail to Abalone Point, where the Yurok tribe once had a seasonal village. (The steep spur descends to oceanside fishing and diving access—⅛ mile round trip.)

The Rim Trail turns southeast, crossing three small bridges. At 1⅜ miles you meet a paved trail from Abalone Campground. Turn right onto the paved trail and cross a bridge over Penn Creek, coming to another junction. The paved trail continues to the Campfire Center. On your left is your return trail to the trailhead. But unless your time or energy is running short, go right to one last magnificent viewpoint: Palmer's Point.

You follow Penn Creek for 100 feet, then bend left. Just beyond 1½ miles you cross a bridge over Beach Creek and head west. The trail passes through dense forest of Sitka spruce, shore pine and Bishop pine. The trail bed ends at 1¾ miles at the paved road to Palmer's Point. Walk the road for ⅛ mile to its end where a picnic area has a wonderful view up and down the coast. One spur trail leads west to the end of Palmer's Point. Another forks north to descend to rocky Cannonball Beach, a popular tide pooling spot.

Now retrace your steps back to the Penn Creek bridge. Do not cross the bridge, but instead take the trail that leads east, heading upstream with the creek on your left. Soon you cross a paved road. At 2½ miles you cross Penn Creek and come to a fork. Bear left to return to the trailhead.

The trail climbs gradually through dense spruce forest, turning north as it crosses six small bridges. You cross the main park entrance road just east of the entrance station.

Now follow the signs that say Park Headquarters. Cross Ickie Ughie Creek and meet another fork at 2⅞ miles. You can take the right fork here to Park Headquarters, then walk the road back to your trailhead. I prefer to take the left fork, which passes by the Red Alder Group Picnic Area, then meets a trail to Ceremonial Rock. At 3 miles the trail forks again, with the left fork climbing to the top of Ceremonial Rock in ⅛ mile. To return to the trailhead, take the right fork, which is marked Agate Beach Campground.

You come to coastal prairie, then cross a road. Descend to a bridge over Beaver Creek and ascend to a restroom in Agate Beach Campground. Go northeast on the campground road to return to the parking area at the trailhead.

TRINIDAD STATE BEACH

The town of Trinidad is the oldest in Humboldt County and, with a population of 350, one of the smallest incorporated cities in the state. The history of habitation here goes back much farther. The Yurok village of Tsurai, their largest coastal village, was located on the north shore of Trinidad Bay. Archaeological evidence shows it was inhabited continuously for over 1000 years, perhaps much longer. This southernmost village of the Yuroks was occupied until 1916.

Spanish explorers entered the bay on Trinity Sunday in 1775, naming it and claiming it for Spain. Russian fur trappers visited several years later. The Josiah Gregg party stopped here on December 7, 1849, carving the latitude and date into a tree. They named it Gregg's Point, unaware of the previous Spanish discovery.

As the gold fever grew in California, ships left San Francisco searching for the protected harbor described by Gregg's party. Three schooners finally succeeded in March, 1850.

A month later streets were laid out, temporary buildings erected, and 140 people voted in the first election. By July Trinidad boasted 300 residents and opened a trail to the Klamath and Trinity mines. A sawmill opened in 1852. But as Eureka and Arcata grew, Trinidad's star faded. Still, a lighthouse was established in 1871 and the town boomed briefly again as a whaling port in the 1920s. Today the sleepy little city on a marine terrace caters mostly to tourists and fishermen, not miners and whalers.

The charm of Trinidad State Beach lies in its wildness. Although its 159 acres are within and adjacent to town, the short, easy trails transport you to a rugged and wild shoreline with spectacular views.

24A.

ELK HEAD/COLLEGE COVE
WILD GARDEN AND SHORE

The Elk Head Trail leaves from the north end of the unpaved north parking area. The trail heads northwest through coastal scrub and grasslands, quickly turning west onto the broad promontory of Elk Head. The tall shrub cotoneaster grows here with its attractive red berries, as do Sitka spruce, red alder and the endangered western lily. The Columbia lily and black crowberry reach their southern limit here. Your trail descends gradually, approaching the southern shore of the headland. At ⅛ mile a side trail on the left descends by many steps to the north end of the beach at College Cove. The Elk

ELK HEAD AND COLLEGE COVE:

DISTANCE: ⅞ mile or 1½ mile semi-loop.

TIME: One hour.

TERRAIN: Level headland to grass- and scrub-covered promontory. Possible tide pooling and walk on beach.

ELEVATION GAIN/LOSS: Less than 100 feet to Elk Head. To College Cove: 100 feet-/100 feet+

BEST TIME: Spring, early summer. Medium to low tide for beach.

WARNINGS: Watch for poison oak. Stay back from edge of cliffs.

DIRECTIONS TO TRAILHEAD: Exit Highway 101 at Trinidad, M.100.7 from north, M.100.5 from south. Go west on Main Street, then right on Trinity Street (which becomes Stagecoach Road) for .7 mile and turn left into unpaved parking lot. Trail leaves from north end.

FURTHER INFO: Trinidad Chamber of Commerce (707) 677-3448.

OTHER SUGGESTION: A HORSE TRAIL leaves from west end of parking area and winds south to Mill Creek and Trinidad Beach.

Head Trail continues west and level onto a flat-topped promontory. This is a marine terrace, ancient ocean floor uplifted by the geological forces which continue to shape this coast. Dense clumps of salmonberries and thimbleberries grow along the trail.

At ¼ mile the coastal scrub opens up on your left. Take a few steps to the edge of the bluff for a spectacular view of College Cove, Pewetole Island and Trinidad Head. After your trail turns southwest, you leave the scrub for grasslands with scattered pockets of low scrub.

Your trail leads to bluff's edge at ⅜ mile. Just below you is jagged Omenoku Point. A brushy fisherman's trail leads down to the point, but your trail bends right to scrub-covered Elk Head and Megwil Point.

Just before ½ mile, the trail makes a big right bend. Here, near the tip of Elk Head, another side trail on your left heads northwest, then north for ⅛ mile to the tip of Megwil Point, where you get a glimpse of the coast to the north. Offshore sits Green Rock, with one of the state's largest colonies of common murres, 16-inch tall, black and white seabirds of the auk family. The population of tiny Green Rock is estimated at 55,000 murres! To the southwest is Flatiron Rock, home to 24,000 more murres and five other bird species, as well as seals and sea lions. At low tide you can descend the rocks to excellent tide pools at Megwil and Omenoku Points. Be careful!

The main trail turns east, making a short loop. Shore pine, Sitka spruce and cypress grow here. Scattered pockets of heather also grow here, some climbing on other vegetation to heights of 8 feet. At ⅝ mile you rejoin the main trail. Continue east just ¼ mile to your car.

You may prolong your hike with a walk on College Cove Beach. To do this, take the side trail ⅛ mile from the trailhead. It descends by 100 rough steps to the north end of the beach. You can walk southeast on the beach for ¼ mile, although at high tide you must scramble over a pile of boulders. South of the rockpile, the sandy beach continues. A beautiful, large specimen of coast silktassel grows just above the beach. A small waterfall lies just beyond. Return by the same route to your trailhead.

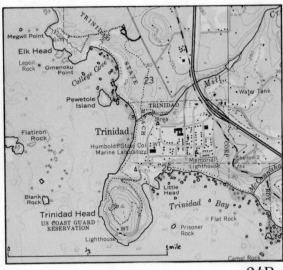

24B.

MILL CREEK TO BEACH
TO THE FOOT OF PEWETOLE ISLAND

The paved southern parking area lies within the city limits of Trinidad. A pleasant picnic area with restrooms and piped water is on a lawn-covered hillside. The Mill Creek Trail to Trinidad Beach starts from here, passing to the right of the restrooms.

The trail heads north, then descends by switchbacks into Sitka spruce, grand fir and red alder forest. You descend

DISTANCE: ½ mile, round trip to beach.
Full hike: 1⅜ miles, round trip.

TIME: One hour.

TERRAIN: Descend along Mill Creek to Trinidad Beach.
Beach walking to south, tide pooling to north.

ELEVATION GAIN/LOSS: 160 feet-/160 feet+, round trip.

BEST TIME: Low tide. Spring.

WARNINGS: Do not get trapped by the rising tide. Watch for
rogue waves on beach.

DIRECTIONS TO TRAILHEAD: Exit Highway 101 at Trinidad, M.100.7 from the north, M.100.5 from the south.
Go west on Main Street, then right on Trinity Street for
one block to the paved parking area on left.

FURTHER INFO: Trinidad Chamber of Commerce (707)
677-3448.

above the creek, crossing two boardwalks before coming to a
rest bench with a pleasant view of Mill Creek Canyon. The
lush understory includes redwood sorrel, blue flag iris,
piggyback plants, sword ferns and ivy.

At ⅛ mile a giant evergreen huckleberry towers over the
trail. You continue a gradual descent, paralleling the creek.
The forest soon gives way to coastal scrub with blackberry,
bush lupine, plantain and coltsfoot. You come to a rest
bench with an expansive view of the beach, Trinidad Head
and wooded Pewetole Island just offshore.

The trail turns right and descends steps to a junction with
a horse trail. (If you turn right, it is ¾ mile to the northern
parking area. See Trail #24A.) Go left at the junction and
drop to the beach at the mouth of Mill Creek, ¼ mile from the
trailhead. You can walk the broad beach south for ⅜ mile to
the base of Trinidad Head, where you can turn east and walk
city streets back into town if you wish. Or you can return the
way you came.

The beach north of the creek's mouth is best at low tide. At
a tide of -1.0 feet or better, you can walk west about 400 feet,
then walk northwest to the base of Pewetole Island. This
steep rock island has a heavily forested top. Black oyster-
catchers nest there. This 17-inch-high black bird has a long
red bill for prying shellfish from the rocks.

If you are here at low tide, be careful that the rising tide
does not block your return.

MORE TRINIDAD TRAILS

The Trinidad area is a paradise for the hiker who likes short and scenic seaside trails. In addition to the trails of Patrick's Point State Park and Trinidad State Beach, the trails described below provide access to the spectacularly rugged coast and beaches.

25.

TSURAI LOOP ON TRINIDAD HEAD
CLIMB HIGH ABOVE THE PACIFIC

Park your car at the beach parking lot at the west end of Edwards Street. East of the lot, a sign marks the start of the Trinidad Head trails (day use—no vehicles except Coast Guard beyond that point). The trail starts as a narrow paved road that climbs for the first ⅛ mile, with views of the steep east side of Trinidad Head, the harbor and Prisoner Rock just offshore, and the rocky coast to the south. You then pass through a gate in the fence around the Coast Guard Reservation.

After the gate, the road climbs through dense coastal scrub as the hill steepens. At ¼ mile, as you come to a big bend left, a dirt trail leaves the road heading west. Benches at the start of the path provide views north to Trinidad Beach, Pewetole Island and Elk Head. Take the dirt trail, descending 4 steps, then climbing to more benches with grand views. Just beyond those benches, a side trail forks right. It descends in 500 feet to more view benches at the base of a rock outcrop.

Beyond the fork the main trail climbs southeast. You pass many berry vines that flower in March and April and bear fruit from June through September. The moderately steep

TSURAI LOOP ON TRINIDAD HEAD:

DISTANCE: 1½-mile loop.

TIME: One hour.

TERRAIN: From sea level, climb through coastal scrub on the promontory of Trinidad Head to a rock outcrop 300 feet above the Pacific, then loop back to starting point.

ELEVATION GAIN/LOSS: 300 feet+/300 feet-

BEST TIME: Spring. Any clear day.

WARNINGS: Watch for traffic on paved road. Watch for poison oak on trail.

DIRECTIONS TO TRAILHEAD: Exit Highway 101 at Trinidad, M.100.7 from north, M.100.5 from south. Go west on Main Street, then left on Trinity Street to its end. Go right on Edwards and descend to beach parking area. Trail starts to the east.

FURTHER INFO: Trinidad Chamber of Commerce (707) 677-3448.

trail switches left, then to the right before ⅜ mile. You level and come to more benches; this is a good whale-watching spot when gray whales are migrating, December through April. Look beyond the buoy for their spouts.

Your trail climbs again, heading south. Ahead you see your destination, a high rocky point. Climb through a thicket of silktassel to another rest bench at ½ mile. Unless it is very windy or foggy, take the side trail on the right. The short spur climbs steps to the top of the rock outcrop on the western edge of Trinidad Head. You are 300 feet above the Pacific, with views in every direction. Although you are about 60 feet below the summit of Trinidad Head, the view from here is more expansive than the view from the top. Pilot Rock, due south of here, was used by early explorers to locate and navigate the entrance to Trinidad Bay.

When you get enough of the view, descend to the main trail and head south through a pocket of lush vegetation where cow parsnips abound. Soon, another short spur on the right leads to a view down the steep southwest face. The main trail switches left and climbs again, switching right in 150 feet. You pass through tall coastal scrub dominated by wax myrtle. Another view bench looks south at ⅝ mile. On a clear day you can see Cape Mendocino.

Your trail levels, passing a mountain beaver den and more tall scrub. You quickly come to a large granite cross marking where the Spanish explorers placed a wooden cross during their visit in 1775. Two benches overlook the coast and a grove of large Sitka spruce growing on the south face below.

Now head north toward the microwave station at the summit. At ¾ mile you come to a gravel road. Turn right on the road and descend toward town. You can see boats anchored in Trinidad Bay below. To the east lie Houda Point and Little River Rock.

At ⅞ mile you pass another bench and switch right. You bend back to the left at one mile and meet the paved road. Go left on the pavement, making a gradual descent past several rest benches with fine views of Prisoner Rock, Trinidad Harbor, Little Head and Indian Beach.

At 1¼ miles your descent steepens. You bend right, completing your loop as you pass the dirt trail on the left. Descend along the paved road to return to your car, a total hike of 1½ miles.

26.

INDIAN BEACH

EASY TO REACH SECLUDED BEACH

Walk east on Wagner Street past the first house on the right. The trail heads south toward Trinidad Bay from there. In 100 feet you come to a plaque inscribed "Indian Beach Trails— The Humboldt North Coast Land Trust and the Citizens of Trinidad." The trail turns left at the plaque. Follow the grassy trail 500 feet, to where it turns south toward the beach, passing between alders and Sitka spruce. You descend a total of 92 steps, then cross a gravel driveway and descend to the beach before ¼ mile.

You can walk west for ¼ mile along the sand to a pile of boulders at the end of the beach. Fishing and pleasure boats lie at anchor in Trinidad Bay on your left, as you walk west toward Trinidad Head. On your right a thicket of alders and willows gives the beach a secluded feeling, even though you are right next to town. On the bluff above you was once the Yurok village of Tsurai, an important settlement that saw 1000 years of continuous use until 1916. As you return to the east, you have excellent views of the rugged, rocky shoreline to the east and south.

Going east from the trail, you can walk almost ⅜ mile. In 300 feet is a beached sea stack with a grassy top. A rough trail climbs to its top. At ⅛ mile, east of the trail, Indian Beach ends. Unless it is high tide, you can easily scramble over the rocks, where beach silverweed grows. On the far side of the rocks is a rocky tide pool area to explore at low tide.

Stretching to the east is a pebbly beach called He'Woli-Wroi Cove. You can walk this beach to the cliff at its east end, which blocks further progress. As you walk the beach, the many offshore rocks and sea stacks provide spectacularly changing vistas of the rugged coast.

Return to the trail and climb the 92 steps to your car. If you walked to both ends of the beach and back, you hiked 1⅜ miles.

INDIAN BEACH:

DISTANCE: Round trip to beach: ½ mile.
    Total hike: 1⅜ miles.
TIME: One hour.
TERRAIN: Descend to secluded beach right below town. Beach walking and tide pooling.
ELEVATION GAIN/LOSS: 160 feet-/160 feet+, round trip.
BEST TIME: Medium to low tide.
WARNINGS: Do not trespass on adjacent private property.
DIRECTIONS TO TRAILHEAD: Exit Highway 101 at Trinidad, M.100.7 from north, M.100.5 from south. Go west on Main Street, then left on Trinity Street to its end. Go left on Edwards Street for one block. Where it turns left and becomes Ocean Street, park at the corner of Wagner Street.
FURTHER INFO: Trinidad Chamber of Commerce (707) 677-3448.

27

OTHER TRINIDAD TRAILS

SHORT HIKES TO RUGGED COAST

The other Trinidad area trails leave from Scenic Drive, the old portion of Highway 101 which follows the coast south from the main Trinidad exit. They are listed from north to south.

The BAKER BEACH TRAIL leaves the road about .2 mile south of Baker Beach Road. The trail leaves from the north end of the parking area, descending steeply through alder and spruce forest to reach the beach in 350 feet. The beach stretches north for ⅜ mile. After you come to a rocky point, good rocky tidepools lie offshore from the pebbly beach.

The LUFFENHOLTZ BEACH TRAIL leaves from the north end of the large paved parking area for Luffenholtz County Park. It descends steeply west to reach the sandy beach in 300 feet.

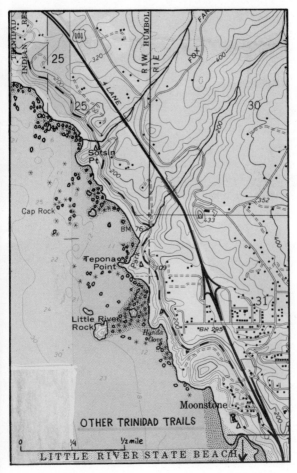

OTHER TRINIDAD TRAILS

LITTLE RIVER STATE BEACH

Another trail from the southwest portion of the parking area leads out onto narrow, scrub-covered Tepona Point, ending in ⅛ mile.

The HOUDA POINT TRAIL leaves from a cypress grove, descending stone steps. In 150 feet the trail forks. The left fork leads to Houda Point; the right fork descends in another 300 feet to a popular surfing beach beside Little River Rock. The flat beach is broad at low tide, narrow to submerged at high tide.

MOONSTONE COUNTY PARK is reached by a side road on the right, descending to a parking area at the beach. There is no developed trail here, just access to the beach. You can walk south along the beach for miles, though you must ford Little River to do it (easy ford in summer and fall, may be deep in winter and spring).

28.

MAD RIVER BEACH AND DUNES

NINETEEN MILES OF UNBROKEN BEACH

The steep and rocky shores running from Del Norte County to Trinidad change abruptly at the mouth of Little River. From there a continuous beach stretches south-southwest for 19 miles to the mouth of Humboldt Bay. Most of it is backed by high and low sand dunes that provide a wild and varied habitat for the adventurous hiker, not to mention shelter for the coastal-strand community of plants.

An ambitious hiker could start south from Moonstone County Park, ford Little River and hike the entire beach. The major obstacle is the crossing of Mad River. This major stream can be easy to ford in late summer or early fall. During the rest of the year, however, one must head east to the Hammond Bicycle Trail, cross the river on Hammond Bridge and return to the beach at Mad River Beach County Park. No obstacles lie from there to the jetty at the mouth of Humboldt Bay.

The hike described here explores the beach and dunes around Mad River Beach County Park. The park includes 150 acres south of the river mouth. It provides access to river and ocean fishing, clamming, hiking, horseback riding and (unfortunately) four-wheeling. No developed trail is here, just acres of beach and dunes to explore; you can keep walking along the beach for as long as time and motivation will permit.

From the parking area follow a jeep trail west-northwest through low dunes. You come to the tide line in about ⅛ mile. Head south along the firm sand just beyond the reach of the waves. By ½ mile the beach becomes broader, and the dunes east of the beach are taller. From the one-mile point, much large driftwood lies along the beach. Sandpipers, sanderlings and curlews feed along the water line.

At 1½ miles a pole stands atop the dune nearest the beach; you can use it as a landmark. You can walk south along the beach for another 11 miles, but the described hike follows the beach for ⅛ mile beyond the pole. Where two large driftwood stumps lie at tide line, a four-wheel-drive track heads east into the dunes. Follow this to the top of the first dune. From there you can see a high dune to your east with a top covered with Sitka spruce.

Look southeast for the tallest dune in that direction. Your route heads cross-country through the dunes for the top of that 75-foot-tall sand hill. As you walk through an area lush with coastal-strand plants, please try not to trample them. Along with dune grass grow yellow bush lupine, sea rocket, beach strawberry and yarrow.

At 2 miles from the trailhead, you are heading up the last incline to the top of the high dune. You reach the top before 2⅛ miles. It provides fine views (unless you are fogbound). An old ranch sits in a lush green valley to the south. Beyond it is the Nature Conservancy's Lanphere-Christensen Dune

MAD RIVER BEACH AND DUNES:

DISTANCE: 4-mile loop or open-ended beach walk.

TIME: At least 2 hours.

TERRAIN: Long, unbroken beach backed by high dunes.

ELEVATION GAIN/LOSS: 125 feet+/125 feet-

BEST TIME: Spring for wildflowers, any day that is not foggy for views.

WARNINGS: Watch for killer waves on beach. You may share the beach and dunes with motorized vehicles. Be aware of them. Poison oak may be found in the dune vegetation.

DIRECTIONS TO TRAILHEAD: Exit Highway 101 onto Janes Road at M.89.05 on north, M.88.9 on south. Go right on Janes for .1 mile, then right on Heindon Road for .4 mile. Go left on Miller Lane for .9 mile. Then go right on Mad River Road. You come to Hammond Bridge after 1.9 miles. The road turns west to reach the parking area and trailhead in 1.1 miles.

OTHER ACCESS TO 19 MILE BEACH: Moonstone County Park: Exit 101 at M.98.05.

Little River State Beach: Exit 101 at M.97.4.

Clam County Beach: Exit 101 at M.95.8.

Also off Highway 255 near Manila and Samoa.

FURTHER INFO: County Parks (707) 445-7652.

OTHER SUGGESTION: MOUTH OF MAD RIVER is 2 miles north. The estuary is used by hundreds of migratory waterfowl and shorebirds. Snowy plovers nest south of the river mouth. You may also see bald eagles, prairie falcons and Aleutian Canada geese.

LANPHERE-CHRISTENSEN DUNE PRESERVE is run by the Nature Conservancy. They lead tours on Saturdays at 10 A.M. (except July and August). Call 822-6378.

THE HAMMOND TRAIL is being developed from Clam Beach to Arcata. Particularly for bikers and equestrians, it crosses the Mad River on the Hammond Bridge, one mile east of Mad River Park. It winds through the beautiful farmlands of the Arcata Bottoms. Call Life Cycle at (707) 822-7755 or Adventure's Edge (707) 822-4673.

Preserve (see *other suggestions*). East of that is Mad River Slough, the ancient mouth of Mad River when it emptied into Humboldt Bay. Beyond the slough lies the north arm of Humboldt Bay. The town of Arcata spreads along its shore. To the east lie the farmlands of the Arcata Bottoms, the Trinity Mountains rising beyond. When it is very clear you can see Trinidad Head to the north.

Your return route goes cross-country through the dunes, heading generally north. Before you leave the high dune, study your route: stay west of the tree-covered dune to the north and head generally toward the left side of a distant stand of trees near the mouth of Mad River.

Descending the high dune, aim for the west side of the spruce-covered dune, which you reach at 2½ miles. Then head for the trees near the river mouth (15 degrees NNE if you have a compass). At 3 miles is a hollow where bush lupine and beach strawberry thrive. Continuing toward the far stand of trees, you encounter dense vegetation. You might want to detour left to find bare sand for easier walking.

At 3¾ miles a big barn lies to your east. Steer wide of it, because it is surrounded by an electric fence. Continue past the left side of the trees and come to the parking lot at 4 miles.

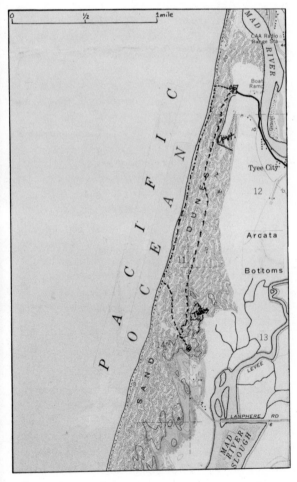

29

ARCATA'S REDWOOD PARK

WITH MODEL COMMUNITY FOREST

*Few city parks have enough trails to be included in hiking
guides, but this is no ordinary city park. Redwood Park and
Community Forest include 600 acres on the north slope of
Fickle Hill, prime redwood-growing land. The City of Arcata
acquired the land through several purchases, starting in
1905. In 1955 it was dedicated—the first municipally owned
forest in the state of California.*

*Today Redwood Park and Community Forest include 10
miles of trails, many of which are available to equestrians
and mountain bikers (see map). Trails are open except when
logging occurs in a particular area. In that case the closure
is posted. The trails are well used by the residents of Arcata,
being no more than a ten-minute walk from downtown or
Humboldt State University.*

*The city is striving to create a model forest. All logging is
done to strict environmental standards. Low-impact,
balloon-tired vehicles are used. Sustained-yield timber
harvesting is the law here. The enhancement of wildlife,
watershed, and aesthetic values of the forest is a primary
goal. Proceeds from logging support recreational facilities in
the city.*

*The loop described below samples the best of the trail
system in the park. Since bikers and equestrians are not
allowed on the first ¾ mile of trail, they should use the
Meadow Trailhead, where 14th Street enters the park.*

The parking area is at the end of 14th Street, where a grassy
field has picnic tables and other facilities. Look across the
field to a sign, "Redwood Park Trails." Climb the steps by the
sign and enter a forest of redwood and Sitka spruce. Your
trail climbs through the forest. At ⅛ mile you encounter the
first of many big stumps left from the logging activities of the
late 1800s. In 200 feet, a canyon lies on the left. The trail
climbs along its edge.

In 300 feet the Short Trail forks right. You return by it at
the end of the described hike. Now go left on the Nature
Trail. Descend across two small bridges. Go left on a bridge
over tiny Campbell Creek, climbing steps on the other side.

You soon descend again, passing a huge stump at ⅜ mile.
Go down the steps and recross the creek. The trail descends
along Campbell Creek. Cross a bridge over a side canyon and
come to a boardwalk at ½ mile. You cross a second boardwalk
and come to a junction.

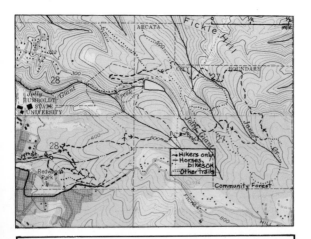

ARCATA'S REDWOOD PARK:

DISTANCE: 6⅛ mile loop.

TIME: 2-4 hours.

TERRAIN: Up and down steep canyons of a north-slope redwood forest.

ELEVATION GAIN/LOSS: 1200 feet+/1200 feet-

BEST TIME: Anytime.

WARNINGS: Bikes and horses restricted (see map).

DIRECTIONS TO TRAILHEAD: Exit Highway 101 at Arcata, on north at Sunset Avenue (M.87.2), on south at Samoa exit (M.85.5). Go to either 11th or 14th Street and go east, following signs to Redwood Park. Main parking area is at end of road.

FURTHER INFO: City of Arcata (707) 822-5953 or 822-3619.

OTHER SUGGESTION: AZALEA STATE RESERVE provides a mile of trails through dense stands of fragrant azalea in spring. Exit McKinleyville South at M.89.8 from south, M.90.1 from north, and go east on North Bank Road.

The end of the Nature Trail is on the left, but our described trail goes right on the Sitka Trail. It descends over boardwalks and bridges to recross Campbell Creek. You can see the old skid, or corduroy, road in the creek bed. Imagine a dozen oxen pulling a giant log down the creek. The trail climbs gradually to some rest benches at ⅝ mile. Descend to meet the Meadow Trail before ⅞ mile. A picnic table sits by the junction. People on horses or bikes should come up the hill to meet the trail here, just ⅛ mile from 14th Street.

From the junction, climb the steep hill to the ¾-mile point, where you go right and continue a moderate climb. You are heading east along the north boundary of Redwood Park. The trail steepens at ⅞ mile, then continues its steady climb beyond one mile. The trail levels briefly in a clearing where redwood violets and other wildflowers grow. You climb gradually to the next junction.

After 1⅛ miles you meet two dirt roads. The second one is Fickle Hill Grade. (You can turn right for a shorter hike of 2 miles.) Go left and head north, passing the Big Rock Trail at 1¼ miles. Follow Fickle Hill Grade as it veers right and heads east, descending slightly. Red-flowering currant, trillium, coltsfoot and iris grow along the trail. Berries include elder-, salmon- and thimbleberries. You climb gradually again from 1⅜ miles.

At 1½ miles you cross a fork of Jolly Giant Creek, then climb steeply to a junction. Fickle Hill Grade ends here, but you continue on the same road surface, now called Community Forest Loop Road. You pass under the power line and climb through an area planted with young trees. Descend to cross Jolly Giant Creek at 1¾ miles.

After the creek you climb north. The trail levels at a junction with the Ridge Road. (You can go left on Community Forest Loop for a shorter hike of 4½ miles.) Our described route goes right on Ridge Road and climbs, passing a spur on the right, then one on the left. After a steep hill, you meet the Upper Janes Creek Trail on the left, which you follow. (You can go right for a loop one mile longer.)

The Upper Janes Creek Trail climbs for 250 feet, then levels. You cross a boardwalk and descend through a swampy area where yellow skunk cabbage thrive. After a brief climb, you descend toward Janes Creek. You come to another swampy area at 2¼ miles and promptly cross tiny Janes Creek. The trail switches left and climbs above the creek. Wild ginger and deer fern thrive in the moist habitat. At 2⅜ miles you switchback right and climb steeply through healthy second-growth forest.

You meet Janes Creek Road at 2½ miles from the trailhead. Turn left and climb through an area recently planted with redwood and Douglas fir seedlings. In 250 feet you reach the summit of your hike, 900 feet in elevation. If you are tired, it might please you to know that most of the return hike is downhill. You descend generally north. Violets, irises and trilliums brighten the path in spring.

You pass several small clearcut areas. After 3⅛ miles your

trail descends generally west, with views of the coast north of Arcata. The sunny clearings along the road provide an ample harvest of berries in summer: red and black huckleberries, blackberries, thimbleberries, salmonberries, salal, currants and Oregon grapes.

At 3⅜ miles you meet the power line cut and descend a steep hill. After you cross Janes Creek, the Lower Janes Creek Trail branches left. Your trail leaves the clearing, crosses a feeder creek, bends right and climbs for ⅛ mile. The trail levels and meets the Vista Road at 3¾ miles. Go left on Janes Creek Road and descend a steep hill. The road then climbs briefly to end at the junction with the Community Forest Loop Road.

You head straight (west). After passing a large water tank, the road descends past the California Trail at 4 miles. You continue a gradual descent, with private houses on the right. On your left is the canyon of Jolly Giant Creek. You bend left at 4¼ miles and descend into the canyon. At an unmarked junction you veer left and head east. (The right fork leads to the HSU campus.)

The trail climbs along Jolly Giant Creek for ⅛ mile, then crosses the earth-fill dam of an old reservoir. You climb through the forest to the Big Rock Cutoff Trail at 4½ miles (hikers can go right for a shorter but steeper route). The Community Forest Loop Road climbs for over ¼ mile before it tops a hill and descends to Fickle Hill Grade at 4⅞ miles.

Turn right and retrace your steps of the early part of the hike, descending to the Meadow Trail at 5¼ miles. Bikers and equestrians should descend the Meadow Trail to the starting point. Hikers stay on Fickle Hill Grade, climbing for 150 feet before descending in a big loop around the lush headwaters of Campbell Creek.

The descent steepens at 5⅜ miles. At 5½ miles you descend gradually around a big bend left, where grand fir mixes with the redwoods. At 5⅝ miles you climb briefly, coming to a water tank, then to Fickle Hill Road. Immediately veer right onto the Short Trail and descend through the forest.

You join the Nature Trail Loop at 5⅞ miles. Go left, returning to the parking area at 6⅛ miles.

30

ARCATA MARSH
AND WILDLIFE SANCTUARY

RESTORED WETLANDS PROVIDE FINE BIRDING

In 1979 the City of Arcata created its Marsh and Wildlife Sanctuary, reclaiming the area along South I Street that had become an industrial wasteland left over from the post-World War II logging boom. The Sanctuary, considered a model wetlands restoration project, serves as an integral part of Arcata's wastewater treatment system.

The city built three freshwater marshes and a lake at the site. They planted the marshes with sedge, sago pondweed and ditch grass, and stocked the lake with rainbow trout. Today the 154 acres of wetlands are a haven for some 200 bird species. Amateur birders find the Saturday morning walks led by local Audubon Society members a wonderful introduction to the birds of the Sanctuary. Salmon and trout raised in the wetlands are used to stock local creeks.

Each year over 100,000 visitors enjoy the many aspects of nature in the Arcata Marsh and Wildlife Sanctuary by bird-watching, walking, jogging, fishing, boating and picnicking—all within seven blocks of downtown Arcata.

The trail starts at the south end of the parking area at the end of I Street. You can see the rotting pilings of the Arcata Wharf, built in 1855, which extended 1½ miles into Humboldt Bay. The trail passes the restroom, heading southeast. The shore of Klopp Lake is on the left, the mudflats of Humboldt Bay on your right. At high tide the mudflats are submerged, but at low tide they are busy with feeding dowitchers, curlews, godwits, willets, egrets, herons, sanderlings and sandpipers. On the lake float surf scoters, cormorants, coots and various gulls (7 or more species) and ducks. On your left at ⅛ mile, you pass benches facing the lake.

At ¼ mile your path bends left. The mouth of Butcher Slough lies on your right, with the sewage treatment plant in the background. The first fork is at ⅜ miles. The path on the left leads to an observation hill overlooking the lake. You continue on the main path, which comes to a "T" intersection at ½ mile. A tree in the salt marsh before you is a common place to spot black-shouldered kites. Marsh wrens also live in the marsh.

Turn left and head west, with the salt-water marsh on your right. You soon come to a fork, where you go straight. (The trail on the left heads onto the rise with scattered Monterey pines and bird blinds.) The main trail comes to a dike at ⅝ mile, which separates the salt-water marsh you have been walking along from the Allen freshwater Marsh ahead.

Your trail gradually bends right and heads northwest, drawing nearer to the freshwater marsh, a great place to spot ducks. Seen here in one day were mallard, pintail, cinnamon teal, shoveler and bufflehead. A bird blind sits facing the freshwater marsh at ¾ mile. In the willow trees along the

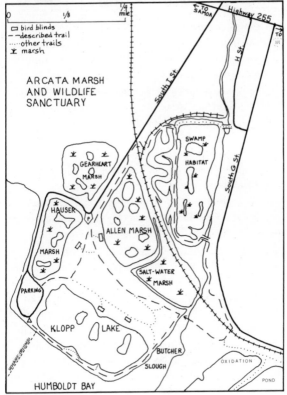

113

DISTANCE: 2-mile loop.

TIME: At least one hour. It is easy to spend hours here when the bird-watching is good.

TERRAIN: Fresh- and salt-water marshlands.

BEST TIME: Audubon-led walks every Saturday at 8:30 A. M.

WARNINGS: Open sunrise to sunset. Be quiet along the trail, or you may be the target of a bird watcher's wrath.

DIRECTIONS TO TRAILHEAD: Exit Highway 101 at M.86.2 from north, M.85.5 from south onto Highway 255 going west. Turn left on I Street. Go to parking area at end of road.

FURTHER INFO: Audubon Society (707) 822-6918. City of Arcata: (707) 822-5951.

OTHER SUGGESTION: ARCATA ARCHITECTURAL TOUR: A morning of birding might well be followed by an afternoon of touring fine old Victorian buildings. Maps of the self-guided tour are available at the Chamber of Commerce, 1062 G Street, (707) 822-3619.

marsh's western edge usually rest at least two dozen black-crowned night herons. You come to a parking area on the paved road. If you take the footpath on the left, it returns to the main parking area for a one-mile loop.

For a longer walk, go right, paralleling the paved road. From this path you can see the Gearheart freshwater Marsh on the left and Allen Marsh on the right. Along the edges of these marshes you may see black phoebes and song and savannah sparrows. Overhead you may spot a belted kingfisher, osprey, harrier (marsh hawk), or, with luck, a peregrine falcon searching for dinner.

You come to the end of the freshwater marshes and cross the railroad tracks, one mile from the trailhead. In 300 feet go right on the Jolly Giant/Butcher Slough Swamp Trail. It crosses a bridge over Butcher Slough, the tidal portion of Jolly Giant Creek (which you crossed if you hiked in the Community Forest). Go right at the fork, along the dike between Butcher Slough on your right and the recently restored swamp habitat on your left. On the elevated dike you have an overview of the entire Arcata Marsh and Wildlife Sanctuary. As you proceed south on the dike, the swamp turns to marsh, then to deeper open water. The changes provide varied habitat for the young salmon and trout raised in the city's aquaculture program.

The path veers left at the end of the pond, crosses a bridge, and goes right, paralleling G Street. At 1½ miles you come to the parking area for the trail to the marsh pilot project and oxidation ponds. Although this loop is not included in the described trail, you can cross the tracks and go left to add about 2½ miles and more opportunities for birding (100 species of birds have been spotted on the ponds or their marshy edges).

Your described trail crosses the tracks and veers right, crossing a bridge over Butcher Slough and joining the first loop at the ½-mile point. You then head west and northwest before taking the path that veers left and heads south near the shore of Hauser freshwater Marsh. You return to the parking lot beside Klopp Lake at 2 miles.

31

ELK RIVER WILDLIFE REFUGE

BIRDS AND WILDFLOWERS WITHIN CITY LIMITS

Elk River is Humboldt Bay's largest tributary. In 1984, after years of farming and industrial development, the City of Eureka restored 100 acres of riparian and marsh habitat near its wastewater treatment plant on the east side of the estuary. Like the Arcata Marsh (see Trail #30), the restored area is open to hiking and bird-watching. It provides a natural habitat amidst the industrial development of Eureka.

The trail heads south from the parking area, following an old railroad grade. On your right is the Elk River estuary, with a large sand spit on its west side. On the left is the Eureka Wastewater Treatment Plant. The trail crosses open grasslands sprinkled with wildflowers in spring and summer.

After ⅛ mile your trail veers left and runs along the fence of the treatment plant. You pass a stand of willow, myrtle and alder, the only tall shrubs in the area. After ¼ mile a marsh lies on the left of the trail. Ducks often take flight as you approach the marsh. Beach strawberry, buttercup, poppy, owl's clover and low-growing ceanothus grow along the trail. A side trail on your left leads to the marsh.

The main trail passes through a thicket of coastal scrub, then returns to grasslands. If you look west as you leave the scrub, you can see the Coast Guard headquarters near the mouth of Humboldt Bay. After ⅜ mile the marsh on your left supports an abundance of cattails. A bush of wild rose grows on the right.

ELK RIVER WILDLIFE REFUGE:

DISTANCE: 1⅜ miles, round trip.

TIME: At least one hour.

TERRAIN: Level ground surrounded by marsh and estuary.

BEST TIME: Spring and early summer for wildflowers. Anytime is good.

WARNINGS: Do not trespass on adjacent private lands. No firearms, vehicles or camping. Pets on leash only.

DIRECTIONS TO TRAILHEAD: Turn west off Highway 101 onto Hilfiker Lane (south end of Eureka at M.75.8). Go .5 mile to parking area to right of entrance to Wastewater Treatment Plant.

FURTHER INFO: City of Eureka (707) 445-3037.

OTHER SUGGESTION: FORT HUMBOLDT STATE HISTORIC PARK is ¼ mile north of Hilfiker Lane on the east side of Highway 101. The fort was established in 1853 to control raids by local Indians. Today there is a small museum, picnic area and wheelchair-accessible restrooms. Call (707) 443-7952.

Just before ½ mile, a second side trail leads to the marsh in 200 feet. The main trail draws nearer the estuary. Much bird life can be seen here, including ducks, egrets and herons in the estuary. Osprey, kites, hawks and northern harriers often hunt overhead.

At ⅝ mile your trail veers left and approaches the railroad tracks. The vegetation is dominated by salt-tolerant plants like cordgrass, pickleweed, hairgrass and northern dune tansy. Two big driftwood logs here make pleasant picnic spots. From here you must return by the same trail to the parking area.

32.

TABLE BLUFF COUNTY PARK
BEACH/DUNE WALK TO MOUTH OF EEL RIVER

The Wiyot tribe inhabited the coastal lowlands from Mad River on the north to the tidelands of Eel River on the south. The tribe came from the Algonquian family, the dominant native stock of eastern and central North America. But their customs followed the Yurok pattern in houses, baskets, canoes and the use of dentalium money.

The Wiyots had two settlements at Table Bluff on the south end of Humboldt Bay—Yachwanawach and Legetku. Legetku was located near the trailhead of this hike. In these villages salt-water fishing and clam digging provided the main food sources. Hunting was of little consequence. Today an Indian rancheria is located on Table Bluff.

In the 1850s settlers, attracted by the rich soil of the bluff, established a small agricultural community, and farming continues today. A lighthouse built on Table Bluff in 1892 served ships entering Humboldt Bay until 1972. Although the lighthouse has been removed, a short trail leads to its site just south of the county park. From that point on a clear day, one has fine vistas north to Humboldt Bay and south to the

TABLE BLUFF COUNTY PARK:

DISTANCE: Up to 9 miles round trip—you choose the distance.

TIME: Plan on 1½ to 2 miles per hour.

TERRAIN: Straight beach backed by low, rolling dunes.

BEST TIME: Spring for wildflowers. Medium to low tide for best walking conditions.

WARNINGS: You may share the beach with off-road vehicles. Do not hike here during hunting season.

DIRECTIONS TO TRAILHEAD: Exit Highway 101 at M.67.9 onto Hookton Road. Follow it west 5 miles to Table Bluff County Park. Follow road for .35 miles more to where it levels at the base of Table Bluff. Park at the big bend.

FURTHER INFO: County Parks (707) 445-7652.

OTHER SUGGESTION: SOUTH SPIT: You can also walk north along the beach, if you do not mind paralleling a paved road. It is about 5 miles to the South jetty.

TABLE BLUFF LIGHTHOUSE TRAIL: A short trail just south of the County Park leads to the site of the old lighthouse.

CRAB COUNTY PARK provides access to more dunes northeast of the Eel River mouth. To get there, turn west off Highway 101 at M.66.3 onto Cannibal Road and go to its end, about 5 miles.

Eel River delta. The persistent winds make the 170-foot cliff at Table Bluff a popular spot for hang gliding.

There is no trail for this hike, just a 4¼-mile-long sand spit between the ocean and the tidal marshlands of the Eel River. The easiest walking is generally on the hard, damp sand near the tide line. But the most interesting part of the area lies in the low dunes east of the beach, near McNulty Slough and North Bay. This is the Eel River Wildlife Area. The described hike follows the beach south and returns through the dunes. You can vary the hike as you prefer.

From the base of Table Bluff, jeep trails lead south through the dunes. Follow the main jeep track for ⅛ mile to the westernmost point of the bluff. Then veer toward the beach on a narrower track that drops to the beach at ¼ mile. The best walking is on the hard sand near the tide line.

Follow the dark sand beach south for at least 2 miles to get to the bays, sloughs and estuaries, the best features here. After 2 miles large stacks of driftwood are along the high tide line. It is just over 4 miles to the mouth of the Eel River. A colony of harbor seals lives on the beach at the river's mouth. The Eel is a reasonable destination for a full-day hike. But keep in mind that walking in soft sand is tiring and that your return hike will probably be against the wind.

Whether you go 2, 3 or 4 miles on the sand spit, head east to explore the low dunes and the shore of North Bay. The dunes shelter beach strawberry, yellow sand verbena, northern dune tansy, sea rocket, bush lupine, purple seaside daisy, silky beach pea and beach morning glory.

Hike back just east of the ridge of the tallest dune where you can find some protection from the wind. Even without a trail, the route provides good walking on mostly hard-packed sand. A four-wheel-drive track winds through the dunes to your east. Its generally loose sand makes poor walking.

One mile north of the river, the mouth of Mosley Slough lies to the east. In another mile you reach the north end of North Bay. It breaks into McNulty and Hawk Sloughs, which swing to the northeast and east, respectively. As you walk through the dunes, you may scare out a black-tailed jack rabbit, the most abundant mammal in Eel River Wildlife Area.

In the 2 miles before Table Bluff, the route along the sand ridge becomes vague. Take your choice of dune, beach or four-wheel track. As long as you head for the left side of Table Bluff, you cannot go wrong.

CENTERVILLE BEACH

Five miles west of Ferndale is four-acre Centerville Beach County Park, providing access to 9 miles of ocean beach. You can walk north to the mouth of the Eel River or south toward False Cape. Dairy farms back the wild beach in the north, steep cliffs in the south. The original stagecoach road from Ferndale to Petrolia, completed in 1871, went through Centerville, followed the beach south before climbing steeply along Oil Creek Ridge, then descended to Capetown.

Today Centerville Beach is open to four-wheel-drive vehicles, so you may have to share the beach and dunes with the whine of gas-powered engines, especially on weekends. But the wild beach can absorb many people and machines before feeling crowded.

33.

CENTERVILLE BEACH NORTH
MORE DUNES AND ESTUARIES BY THE EEL

For walking north along the broad beach from the county park, the best path lies along the firm, moist sand near the tide line. East of the steep wave slope, a flat expanse of sand is riddled with 4-wheel-drive tracks. Low dunes lie east of the tracks.

As you walk north, you pass several driftwood sculptures around ¾ mile. At one mile the beach broadens. From 1½ to 1¾ miles, the lower part of the beach is so steep you cannot see the dunes for the sand bank.

After 2 miles a more gradual slope lies between tide line and dunes. Sandpipers scurry along the water's edge. Cormorants, seagulls and pelicans glide above the surf. Harbor seals may peer curiously from the breakers. On a clear day you can see the abrupt rise of Table Bluff to the north.

The beach cuts in to the east at 3 miles, then cuts in even

CENTERVILLE BEACH—NORTH AND SOUTH:

DISTANCE: North: 11¼-mile round trip.
  South: up to 6¾ miles round trip, depending on tide.
TIME: North: full day. South: 3-4 hours.
TERRAIN: Beach and dune walking.
BEST TIME: Low to medium tide. Spring for wildflowers.
WARNINGS: Heed tide warnings on south hike; do not get trapped by the rising tide. Watch for rogue waves as you walk the beach. Watch for motor vehicle traffic.
DIRECTIONS TO TRAILHEAD: Leave Highway 101 at Ferndale exit M.64.5 on north, M.62.9 on south. Cross Fernbridge and go west 5 miles through town. At south end of Main Steet turn right and go 5 miles to Centerville Beach parking lot.
FURTHER INFO: County Parks (707) 445-7652.

farther at 3¾ miles, where the westernmost dune is only 200 feet from the surf. The dunes stretch north to Table Bluff. A vast wild area of grass and marsh lands lies to the east. To the northeast is the Eel River, with farms along its shore.

The dunes east of the beach are lower after 4 miles. At 4⅝ miles the last high dune lies to the east. At 5½ miles you come to the mouth of the Eel River. Fresh water surges into the ocean here. At high tide, the flow may be reversed. A colony of harbor seals living on the sand bank at the mouth are in prime position to feed on the salmon and steelhead that enter the Eel to spawn.

For the return hike, follow the shore of the Eel River to its confluence with the Salt River in ¼ mile. Then follow the Salt River south, passing the high dune at ⅞ mile. As you walk upriver, the extent and variety of vegetation increases. Beach morning glory and dune grass dominate.

At one mile from the mouth of the Eel, you come to two redwood stumps on the shore of the Salt River, the larger stump being about 8 feet in diameter. Imagine virgin redwood forest extending this close to the mouth of the Eel. In fact, when the first settlers came to Ferndale in 1852, redwood forest covered much of the delta. Some trees were said to be over 400 feet tall. Most of the trees were cut by the 1870s. Barnacles growing on the base of the redwood stump indicate that this land is too wet and brackish to grow redwoods today, suggesting that either this land has sunk since the trees were alive or the river level has risen.

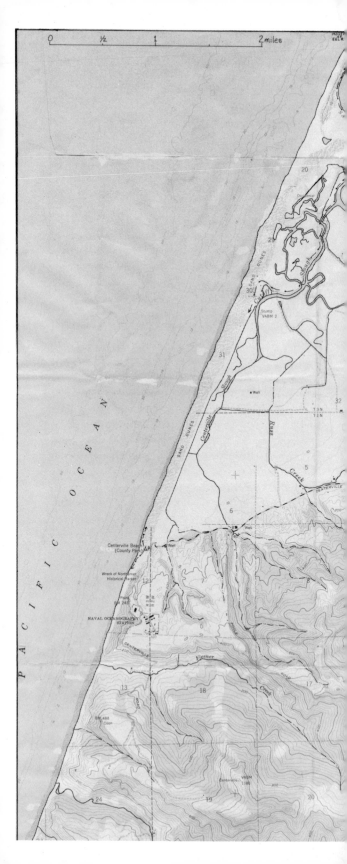

At 1⅛ miles the Salt River estuary splits. Follow the right fork (Cutoff Slough) for ⅛ mile until it splits. Then follow a jeep track along the dry (except at high tide and after heavy rains) channel veering right. At 1½ miles the road splits; take the right fork. It gets sandy, then veers left through loose sand to join a broader track at 1⅝ miles. This heads southwest, then veers back toward Centerville Bluff at 1¾ miles. Dune tansy, beach morning glory, yellow sand verbena and other flowers line your route.

At 2 miles a sign to your east marks a gun club. Egrets and great blue herons congregate beyond the sign. In winter many tundra swans live in these wetlands. From 2¼ miles your route follows an arm of Cutoff Slough. Before 2½ miles your path splits; stay left unless you want to return to the beach. At 2⅝ miles you come to a level, grassy area, then climb onto a levee near a high dune. Head west from here through the dunes to avoid private property surrounding the barn ahead.

After you pass the barn, 3 miles from the Eel River mouth, you can continue on the beach or return to the east edge of the dunes, staying west of private property signs. Beach silverweed, with bright yellow flowers, and lupine grow along the base of the dunes. You approach another barn at 4 miles. Stay west of the barn and fence at 4⅜ miles.

At 4½ miles your path veers right. Trudge through loose sand near the top of the first dune. You may want to return to the beach here because the last mile through the dunes leads through loose sand and an impromptu dune buggy park ¾ mile from the parking area. Come to the parking lot at the county park 5¾ miles from the mouth of the Eel.

34

CENTERVILLE BEACH SOUTH

TOWARD FALSE CAPE

You can also walk south from Centerville Beach County Park. This hike is recommended at a low tide of -1.0 feet or lower. You head south along a beach of pebbly salt-and-pepper sand. From ¼ mile, sandstone cliffs rise to the high bluffs. A stone cross at ⅜ mile memorializes the wreck of the steam schooner *Northerner*. In 1869, en route to the Columbia River, it hit an uncharted rock off Cape Mendocino. Attempting to reach Humboldt Bay, it started sinking off Centerville Beach. Though hundreds of local people came to Centerville to help in the rescue efforts, 38 of the 108 passengers were lost in the stormy seas.

At ½ mile the cliffs rise 240 feet above the beach. At ⅝ mile wire cables descend to the beach from the Naval Oceanography Station on the bluff. Just 250 feet beyond, layers of gray and orange sandstone protrude to the surf. You must have a minus tide in order to continue.

There are two more narrow spots on the beach at the base of soft cliffs of gray sandstone between ¾ and ⅞ mile. You come to the mouth of Fleener Creek at 1⅛ miles. Cattle graze on the grass above the beach.

Walking south, you follow the base of more sculpted gray cliffs. At 1½ miles they reach their highest point, towering nearly 500 feet above the beach. A small waterfall drops 20 feet to the beach at 1¾ miles. Then the beach broadens at the base of a slide area.

Before 2¼ miles you come to a protruding high point, where progress south is blocked at tides higher than -1.0 feet. Do not pass this point unless the tide is low enough and is still ebbing, or else you will not be able to get back around it on your return trip. You may get wet feet even if you wait for a break in the waves. The high cliffs taper to 2⅜ miles where you come to Guthrie Creek.

The mouth of the creek is jammed with driftwood. You can find a sheltered spot for a picnic among the logs. A small lagoon lies between the cliffs at the mouth of the creek. Upstream Guthrie Creek is mostly wooded, unlike the pastures of Fleener Creek.

Just ¼ mile beyond Guthrie Creek, another shelf of gray sandstone protrudes to the surf. You must climb over slippery rocks to proceed. At a tide of -1.0 you are able to walk ¾ mile beyond Guthrie Creek. Even that involves scrambling over several areas of slippery rock. The route south is safely passable only at the lowest tides of the year: -1.5 feet or lower. The mouth of Oil Creek lies one mile south. Beyond it, the steep promontory of False Cape rises 600 feet. Off-shore lie False Cape Rocks, a rookery for several thousand common murres, pigeon guillemots, Brandt's cormorants and western gulls.

On your return hike, be sure to leave time to get around the protruding rocks at 2¼ miles from the county park before the tide comes in.

35.

RUSS PARK
VERDANT WILDERNESS IN A CITY PARK

Ferndale (founded 1852, population 1512), westernmost city in the continental United States, has remained largely unchanged since the 1890s. Dozens of well-preserved Victorian buildings can be found around town. This haven for artists has many galleries and craft shops along Main Street.

Russ Park lies within the city limits. The 105-acre primitive park has over 50 species of plants and 65 species of birds during various times of the year. The park's 2½ miles of trails lead through dense vegetation on the steep terrain. It feels more like a wildlife and plant sanctuary than a typical city park.

Zipporah Patrick Russ, an early settler, donated Russ Park to the city in 1920 "as a park . . . and a refuge and breeding place for birds."

From the parking area, the Lytel Ridge Trail climbs south into the forest. At 200 feet you come to a wooden trail map. The park's lone picnic table sits on the right. Continue steeply uphill through dense vegetation, passing large Sitka spruce and big leaf maples. Salmonberries and red elderberries tower overhead. You ascend gradually as your trail bends left.

By ¼ mile you climb steadily south again. Then your climb eases, passing through dense thimbleberry thickets. As the path levels briefly, go left at a fork. Your trail winds, climbing again at ⅜ mile. In 200 feet go left at another fork. (Take the right fork for a shorter hike to Zipporah's Pond.)

You climb to ½ mile, where the trail tops a ridge and forks into three paths. The two paths on the right are rather overgrown. The right fork leads to Zipporah's Pond and the Bluff Creek Trail. You can follow it now if you prefer a shorter loop of 1½ miles. The described trail takes the left fork to make the ¾-mile Francis Creek Loop, which will return to this point by the center path.

RUSS PARK:

DISTANCE: 2⅛-mile double loop.

TIME: At least 2 hours.

TERRAIN: Climbing a steep, lush coastal ridge from bottom to top and back.

ELEVATION GAIN/LOSS: Full double loop: 700 ft+/700 ft- Lytel Ridge/Bluff Loop only: 460 feet+/460 feet-

BEST TIME: Spring is heavenly. Summer and fall good too.

WARNINGS: No motor vehicles or bikes allowed. Open 6 A.M. to dusk. Watch for poison oak and nettles along trail. Trails are slippery and muddy after rain. Steep terrain; take it easy.

DIRECTIONS TO TRAILHEAD: Exit Highway 101 at Ferndale (M.64.5 on the north, 62.9 on the south). Cross Fernbridge and go west 5 miles through town. At south end of Main Street go left on Ocean Street. It is .75 mile to Russ Park. (Dirt parking on right.)

FURTHER INFO: City of Ferndale (707) 786-4224.

OTHER SUGGESTION: FERNDALE WALKING ARCHITECTURAL TOUR is a self-guided tour of the city's fine Queen Anne, Eastlake, Gothic Revival and Italianate style buildings. Maps are available at the Ferndale Museum, 515 Shaw Ave. (707) 786-4466.

The left fork levels and heads southeast along a ridge. On your right is a steep, wooded canyon. The left side of the trail is covered with false lily of the valley and Douglas iris. As you bend to the right, you climb steeply. At ⅝ mile you bend right again and the climb eases.

The trail forks in 300 feet. The left fork climbs to the highest point in the park, a grassy knob in its southeast corner (elevation 660 feet) with views across the floodplain of the Eel River. The main trail is the right fork. It levels and meets the ridge in 200 feet. You follow the ridge, descending gradually to ¾ mile, then more steeply.

The main trail switches north, then returns to the ridge briefly as you descend by several more switchbacks. After ⅞ mile you leave the ridge for good, descending north, then northeast. Watch out for uneven footing on this section.

At one mile you are descending into a shady canyon. You pass a grand fir of 8-foot diameter. Then switch left on a fern-shrouded section of trail. As you bend left again, the path heads down the center of the canyon. In just 100 feet you come to a fork. Straight ahead, the trail to Francis Creek quickly comes to private property. Take the right fork, climbing gradually northwest. Watch for poison oak here.

The trail switches to the right before 1⅛ miles, climbing through sword ferns by several more switchbacks. At one of these bends grows a western red cedar two feet in diameter. This represents the southern reach of its range. (In Washington, where it is a major forest tree, it reaches heights of 200 feet.) You climb more switchbacks to complete the Francis Creek Loop at 1¼ miles.

Now take the fork on your left. The overgrown trail climbs to overlook green Zipporah's Pond. The trail bends right and descends to the shore in 100 feet. You may smell the giant skunk cabbage at the pond before you see them.

The pond nestles in a hollow in the Sitka spruce forest. Skunk cabbage grows in the shallows. The entire surface of the pond is covered with duckweed. This is a special spot, very tranquil, with only the chirp and buzz of birds and insects. Sedge, ferns, coastal manroot, morning glory and

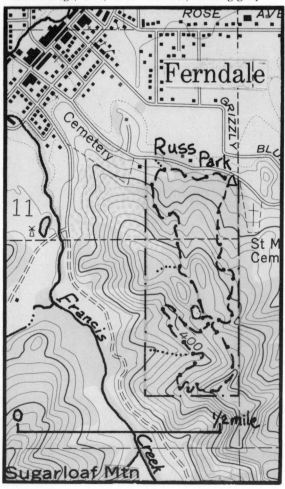

alder line the shore. Berries include evergreen a...
huckle-, thimble-, salmon-, and red elderberry.

Take the trail heading north along the shore of t'...
On the north shore is William Crane Grove. The ...
Sitka spruce and alder are native; the redwoods we...
as seedlings and watered by hand for years. The gr...
a wonderful picnic spot. Please keep it clean!

The trail continues north, climbing a hill a...
Scotch broom 15 feet tall. At a fork, the path on t...
to a point where the village of Ferndale lies 50...
like a storybook town. Continuing on the ma...
soon descend steeply. Watch for rough spots i...
1½ miles the descent eases briefly; star solon...
grow along the trail. You soon come to a fence...
Behind it is a steep drop into Bluff Creek Ca...

The trail makes a moderately steep, wi...
through dense salal and sword ferns. It leve...
miles, then makes a side hill descent into the ca...
out for stinging nettles growing tall along this section o...
trail. Watch your step, too; the dense vegetation may obs-
cure the uneven tread on this steep descent.

At 1¾ miles you descend through dense vegetation. A
stand of native hazelnut bushes arches gracefully overhead,
and elderberries, thimbleberries and nettles also tower above
you. Ripe salmonberries maybe found as early as April, as late
as August.

The trail switches left, then right, as it becomes steep and
slippery. At 1⅞ miles you enter a fragrant eucalyptus grove.
In 100 feet a trail on the left leads to the road but not to the
parking area. (You can exit the park here if you walked from
town.) The main trail veers right, climbs through a moist
area and back into spruce forest at 2 miles. You descend
through another salmonberry patch, then level in spruce
forest again. Descend by rough steps, then descend steeply
without steps. As you head uphill again, watch for poison
oak. You descend steeply into a dense brush thicket and
break out into the parking area at 2⅛ miles.

36.

CAPE MENDOCINO
DRIVE AND BEACH WALK

*Cape Mendocino rises dramatically from the Pacific to reach
a 1200-foot summit in less than a mile. The sparsely settled,
windblown Cape is the westernmost point of land on the
Pacific Coast south of Alaska. The prominent Cape and its
hazardous, rock-strewn coast were first charted in 1543 by*

the crew of the Manila galleons of Cabrillo's expedition, returning from the Philippines to Mexico with silk and other oriental treasures. Appropriately, they dubbed it Cabo de Fortunas—Stormy Cape or Cape of Perils. It was given its present name in the 1580s in honor of the viceroy of New Spain, Lorenzo Suarez de Mendoza.

The rugged cape has been a major landmark for coastal navigators ever since. The wind-whipped waters off the cape are among the most dangerous in the Pacific Ocean, with rocks, reefs and shoals often shrouded in dense fog. Although a lighthouse was established on Cape Mendocino in 1868, more than 200 shipwrecks off its shore took dozens of lives from 1850 to 1950. The Japanese Navy torpedoed an American steamship off the Cape in 1941, claiming 5 lives.

Nearly all the steep, rolling grasslands of Cape Mendocino are privately owned, but a paved public road leaves from Ferndale on the north (or Honeydew on the south) to explore the remote ridges, valleys and coastline. The 28 miles from Ferndale to Petrolia lack towns, lodgings or gas stations; they provide some of the most lovely pastoral scenes in California. You have the bonus of access to a wild 4 miles of beach south of Cape Mendocino.

Just south of the hamlet of Petrolia (gas, food, supplies), this route provides hiking access to the north end of 25 miles of wilderness beach, the Lost Coast of King Range National Conservation Area (see Trail #41).

CAPE MENDOCINO:

DISTANCE: Drive: 66 miles Ferndale to Petrolia to South Fork.
  Beach hike: 8 miles or more, round trip.
TIME: Drive: Plan 4 hours minimum. Beach hike: 1 to 5 hours.
TERRAIN: Steep winding drive with access to a wild, windswept beach.
BEST TIME: Spring; fall is next best.
WARNINGS: Drive slowly and enjoy the scenery. Walking on the beach, watch for oversized waves and do not get cut off by the rising tide. Do not trespass on adjacent private property.
DIRECTIONS TO TRAILHEAD: Take Ferndale Exit at M.64.5 from north, M.62.9 from south on Highway 101. Follow signs across Fernbridge and go 5 miles to south end of Main Street. Go right on Ocean Street, then left on Mattole Road. Description starts there.

The Mattole Road heads south from the charming Victorian village of Ferndale. It climbs steeply above the flat Eel River delta. In 6 miles you come to "Malfunction Junction," where Bear River Ridge Road forks left. You have climbed to 1800 feet. The Road winds along the ridge, passing ranches and fields. At 7 miles, a clearing affords views north to Humboldt Bay and Trinidad Head.

After 13 miles your road makes a winding descent into Bear River Valley. The rolling hills have the look of the Scottish Highlands. Capetown Ranch, south of the river, was once a stagecoach stop. After the ranch, the road climbs Cape Ridge, passing a huge lily pond west of the road.

The Mattole Road tops Cape Ridge at 980 feet, then descends steeply, with wonderful views of the cape and the coast. You approach sea level at the mouth of Singley Creek, ½ mile south of the cape, 18 miles from Ferndale.

The road follows the level coast for 6 miles. For hikers, the best all-tide access is 6 miles south at McNutt Gulch. If your visit coincides with a low tide, the northern half of the beach may be passable. You can reach it from the unnamed creek one mile south of Singley Creek. Park at the north end of the bridge and walk 200 feet down the steep creek to the beach.

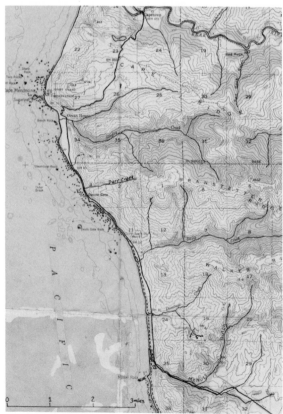

At low tide you can walk north 1¼ miles to the foot of the cape, or south to Devil's Gate. You can also reach the beach from two parking spots at Devil's Gate, 20 miles from Ferndale, but you need a low tide to head north or south.

You cross three more creeks as you drive south from Devil's Gate. The third is McNutt Gulch, where the road turns inland to climb the gulch on its way to Petrolia. At M.23.3 a path leads through the fence to the dunes and beach. You can walk north for 4 miles along the beach, with inspiring views of the rugged Cape and 323-foot Sugarloaf Island. Steamboat Rock, Hell Gate and hundreds of lesser rocks provide breeding areas for seabirds and Steller sea lions. From the McNutt Gulch trail, you can also walk south for up to 3 miles, depending on the tide.

Continuing on Mattole Road, you enter Petrolia in 5 miles. A store and cafe offer provisions, while a steepled church and an old wooden schoolhouse add charm to this pastoral hamlet named for California's first oil boom. Occurring in the 1860s, the boom died after little success.

One mile beyond the store you cross the Mattole River and come to Lighthouse Road, which provides access to the Lost Coast's 25 miles of wilderness beach (see Trail #41).

Mattole Road turns east along the river for which it is named. In 6 miles, A. W. Way County Park lies on the right on a big bend of the river. The park is truly AWAY from the cares of the world. It provides swimming and fishing in the Mattole and picnic and camp spots for reasonable fees.

If you follow Mattole Road 8 more miles, you come to the Honeydew Store, where Mattole Road and Wilder Ridge Road meet. The store, a popular local hangout, is open 9 to 5, Monday through Saturday. It is 23 miles farther on the Mattole Road to reach Highway 101 at South Fork, in the heart of Humboldt Redwoods State Park. The steep, winding road takes one hour. Or you can drive south along Wilder Ridge Road for more access to the King Range (see Trails #41 through 47).

HUMBOLDT REDWOODS
STATE PARK

*Northern California's largest state park (51,234 acres)
stretches along Highway 101 for 40 miles, from south of
Scotia on the north, to Phillipsville on the south. Most of the
park's spectacular redwood groves are accessible by car or
short walks. The 33-mile-long Avenue of the Giants brings
visitors through grove after grove of virgin giants. This
world-famous scenic drive is highly recommended, but to
experience the essence of these primeval forests, hike into
the backcountry away from Highway 101. The more zealous
hiker can take a full day to climb to the top of Grasshopper
Peak or get a permit to sleep overnight in the backcountry at
one of six trail camps in the Bull Creek basin.*

37.

HIKER'S GUIDE TO
THE AVENUE OF THE GIANTS

*Every year three-quarter million visitors from around the
world come to see the Avenue of the Giants, but many never
venture more than ¼ mile from their cars. Although they see
many beautiful redwoods, they never experience the grandeur and solitude of a redwood grove away from the sounds
of roaring traffic. Yet numerous trails lie along Avenue of the
Giants. For further information about these trails, refer to*
Humboldt Redwoods Trail Guide *(revised 1988), available at
the park's Visitor Center for $1.*

On the north, the Avenue of the Giants begins at the Pepperwood exit from Highway 101, at M.46.0 (if you are coming from the south, read the listings from bottom to top).
Pass through the tiny town of Pepperwood. Leaving town
you come to the following features at the markers indicated:
M.43.8. Drury and Chaney Trail on the west side of the road.
   The 2¼-mile semi-loop leads through virgin forest with a
   lush understory of lady fern, oxalis, star solomon seal,
   hazel and poison oak.
M.43.6. Percy French Loop Trail on west side of road. The
   ½-mile loop leads to dedicated groves and the Girdled
   Tree.
M.43.3. Freeway access.
M.40.0. The tiny town of Redcrest.
M.39.65. Freeway access. Then the milepost markers jump
   to M.24.

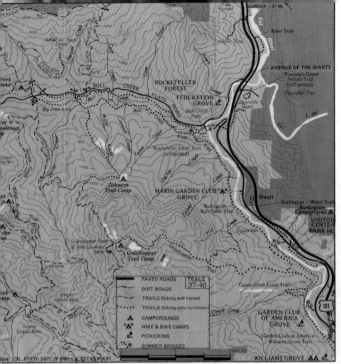

M.22.12. Five Allens' Trail on west side of road. In its 2¼-mile round trip, the trail passes through a tunnel under the freeway and climbs 1000 feet. The trail through mixed forest provides an abundant huckleberry harvest in September and mushrooms after the rains.

M.20.8. Junction with Honeydew Road, which provides access to Trails #38-43. Freeway access going south.

M.20.5. Go east .1 mile to the Founder's Grove Nature Trail, one of the most beautiful and popular hikes in the park. The ½-mile loop is level enough for wheelchairs, although it gets a bit uneven after the Dyerville Giant, the tallest tree in Humboldt Redwoods State Park. Freeway access going north. Avenue of the Giants then crosses to the west side of the freeway.

M.19.6. Road on west leads to California Federation of Women Grove, with a short trail and a picnic area. In summer a bridge across the river leads to Lower Bull Creek Flats.

M.18.17. Gravel trail on west leads into Marin Garden Club Grove, location of the hike/bike campground.

M.18.0. Road on east leads to town of Weott and to freeway.

M.17.55. Parking on west for Gould Bar—fishing and swimming.

M.16.6. Burlington Campground (year-round) to the east. Between campsites 24 and 25 the Burlington Beach Trail follows Robinson Creek to reach the river in ⅜ mile. You can fish year-round (with a license) or spot wildlife at dawn or dusk. In summer the swimming is great, and a low water bridge leads to miles of trails on the west side of the river. Branching left off the Beach Trail is the Fleischmann Trail, which parallels the river for ⅝ mile and includes a self-guiding nature loop.

M.16.5. Humboldt Redwoods State Park Visitor Center includes a museum and small store with postcards and nature guidebooks.

M.15.0 Short loop trail to William Kent Grove on west.

M.14.73. Road on west leads to Garden Club of America Grove. In summer (usually May through September), a low-water bridge crosses the river, providing access to the beautiful Canoe Creek Loop Trail, a 2-mile loop through virgin redwoods in a steep stream canyon rich with wildlife. On the west side of the river, a trail leads north, paralleling the river all the way to Bull Creek Flats (5¼ miles). The River Trail also runs south. Just north of the Canoe Creek Loop, another trail heads west. This is the Grasshopper Trail, which climbs to Grasshopper Peak in 6 miles.

M.13.5. Road on west leads into Williams Grove, which has picnic tables and restrooms. In summer only, a bridge crosses the South Fork of the Eel and connects with the Children's Forest Loop Trail, a 2.4-mile round trip through both young- and old-growth forests. In one mile the Avenue of the Giants passes through the town of Myers Flat. There is access to the freeway as you pass under 101 and head east.

M.11.7. Hidden Springs Campground on left (open May-September). A trail leaves from the campground and goes west to Williams Grove, 1¾ miles. A short trail to Hidden Springs Beach is opposite the campground entrance.

M.8.0. (approximate) The Dry Creek Horse Trail is on the east side of the road, just north of Dry Creek bridge.

M.6.80. Town of Miranda.

M.4.83. Freeway access.

M.4.07. Franklin Lane Grove marks the southern end of Humboldt Redwoods State Park. A short trail leads into the grove, where there is a picnic area. In one mile the road passes through Phillipsville. It passes the Chimney Tree and Hobbittown before joining Highway 101.

38.

BULL CREEK FLATS

Bull Creek acquired its name in the 1860s as the hinterlands of Humboldt County opened to settlement. A settler who lived on the Eel River became one of the first white men to explore Bull Creek when one of his bulls wandered from the herd. He named the pristine creek hidden among immense redwoods after the animal that led him there. Bull Creek was settled in the next decade but the settlers had difficulty with raids by Indians, mountain lions and grizzly bears.

In the summer of 1917, three prominent conservationists, Madison Grant, Henry Osborn and John Merriam, drove the new Redwood Highway through Humboldt County. Camping at Bull Creek, they heard the sounds of logging filtering through the immense redwoods around them. They returned home determined to preserve the tall trees in parklands. In 1918 they established the Save-the-Redwoods League. In 1921 the League purchased its first grove, now a part of Humboldt Redwoods State Park.

John D. Rockefeller Jr. brought his family to see Bull Creek Flat in 1930. Rockefeller's two-million-dollar donation to the League in 1931, matched with state funds, purchased 9000 acres at Bull Creek.

As logging accelerated after World War II, the headwaters of Bull Creek were heavily logged. With the record rains of 1955, the creek became a raging silt- and gravel-filled torrent

BULL CREEK FLATS:

DISTANCE: Up to 8 miles or more, round trip.

TIME: 1-4 hours.

TERRAIN: Mostly level through forest of immense redwoods.

ELEVATION GAIN/LOSS: One way: 200 feet+/240 feet- Round trip: 440 feet+/440 feet-

BEST TIME: Anytime.

WARNINGS: Watch for poison oak.

DIRECTIONS TO TRAILHEAD: Leave Highway 101 at South Fork/Honeydew exit, M.36.1. Go west on Bull Creek Flats Road to Grasshopper Road on left after 4.6 miles. Trail on left of Grasshopper Road after 100 feet.

FURTHER INFO: Humboldt Redwoods State Park (707) 946-2311, 946-2366.

300 feet wide, washing away 50 acres of Bull Creek Flats and toppling 525 trees. Such dire effects of upstream logging led to state acquisition of virtually the entire Bull Creek Basin, bringing Humboldt Redwoods State Park to its present size of 51,234 acres. Though upper Bull Creek still shows logging scars, the forest slowly recovers, aided by reforestation and stream clearing.

The following trail explores the virgin forests of Bull Creek. It provides a cool, shady respite from the heat of summer. In winter, however, the virgin forest is like an icebox, though no less beautiful. Whenever you hike it, bring a sweater or heavier protection.

This description starts at the trail's west end, opposite the turnoff for Albee Creek Campground. (You may join the trail at its one-mile point by going over the all-year bridge across the creek at the Big Tree Area.) In summer a low-water bridge provides access to the east end of the trail from Lower Bull Creek Flats, allowing you to start there or make a loop with the north shore trail.

You start from Grasshopper Road, just 100 feet south of Bull Creek Flats Road, heading east beneath redwoods to 10 feet in diameter. The trail meanders the flood plain along Bull Creek; sections may be wet or muddy after rains. You soon approach the cutbank above the edge of the flood plain.

At ¼ mile you climb the cutbank, now right beside the creek. You climb to a view of the creek, then quickly drop back to the flood plain. The trail winds through forest with an understory of tanoak, huckleberry, sword ferns and salal.

At ½ mile you again climb the cutbank. From a clearing near the top at ⅝ mile, you have a fine view of Bull Creek 60 feet below. On the opposite bank tower immense redwoods. Your trail then descends by seven short switchbacks to the flood plain at ¾ mile, encountering the largest trees yet.

Continue along the flat through a blowdown area where wind and age have brought down many giants. You climb over some logs and pass under and through others. At ⅞ mile the trail meanders, encountering ever larger redwoods. Just before one mile you come to the Flatiron Tree. Its amazing shape demonstrates a leaning redwood's ability to buttress itself. This tree is 7 feet thick on one side and 17 feet thick on the broad side.

Stay left and quickly come to the creek and the year-round bridge at the Big Tree Area. A picnic spot lies across the bridge. To continue along the Bull Creek Flats Trail, stay on the south side of the creek, coming to the impressive Giant Tree. Then veer right, returning to deep forest.

As you meander the level flood plain, notice the variety of plants growing on the forest floor: sword fern, bracken fern, redwood sorrel, iris, trillium, salal and calypso orchid. Some trees support healthy vines winding around their trunks—most of it is poison oak: beware!

At 1¼ miles you pass a giant redwood root ball on your left, then approach a small creek. You soon cross Squaw Creek on a rustic bridge atop a fallen log. Another 300 feet brings you to the junction with the Johnson Camp/Grasshopper Peak Trail. Go left on the Bull Creek Trail.

Continuing on the level trail you pass a rest bench, then a burl-encrusted giant. You again approach the cutbank at 1½ miles. Notice that the trees are smaller where the ground steepens. At 2 miles from the trailhead, you cross Miller Creek on another fallen redwood with railings. The redwood forest thins to allow a few Douglas firs to intrude. By 2⅛ miles the forest is exclusively redwood again.

Before 2¼ miles you enter a natural clearing where two old bends of Bull Creek have been bypassed by the present creekbed. This spot makes a pleasant rest stop. The trail approaches the bank of Bull Creek before plunging back into dense forest, passing large redwoods.

At 2½ miles the trail crosses tiny Connick Creek, then follows it for a few hundred feet. At 2⅝ miles your trail cuts through a blown down redwood. Notice that the tree is nearly six feet in diameter here, 150 feet from its base. Our senses are easily overwhelmed by the immensity of this forest!

At 2⅛ miles pass between two redwood giants leaning on each other for support. For ½ mile the trail traverses an area where standing water collects in winter and spring. The dense forest opens up somewhat at 3⅝ miles, where sword ferns blanket the forest floor. At 3⅞ miles cross Tepee Creek. Follow the creek to its confluence with Bull Creek at 4 miles.

Now the trail becomes more difficult to follow. A steep cutbank rises on the right, with Bull Creek directly on the left. Downed logs at the base of a slide hampered progress at press time, though you could scramble past the obstacles and continue on the gravel stream bed. Just ¼ mile beyond, the trail climbs a steep, gravelly slide and rises 80 feet to plunge back into the forest. It is less than one mile from the first slide to the summer bridge at Lower Bull Creek Flat, but ask about conditions before walking east from the mouth of Tepee Creek, especially in winter. Turning back at the mouth of Tepee Creek still makes an 8-mile round trip from Grasshopper Road, 6 miles from Big Tree Area.

39.

GRASSHOPPER PEAK

TREES, TIE HACKS AND VISTAS

This report follows the Johnson Camp Trail from Big Tree Area to the rustic cabins of Johnson Camp, then joins Grasshopper Road to climb Grasshopper Peak, at 3379 feet the highest point in Humboldt Redwoods State Park. This is the shortest, most direct route to the peak, open only to hikers. If you want to ride horses or mountain bikes to the summit, follow Grasshopper Road (starts one mile to the west) for the entire trip, a longer but less steep route.

To reach the peak on a day hike, leave early and take lunch and plenty of water. Plan 7 to 10 hours round trip for the steep hike. An overnight trip, whether you camp at Johnson or Grasshopper Camp, gives you time to linger at the summit and explore the surrounding countryside.

After parking at the Big Tree Area, cross the bridge over Bull Creek and follow the trail east for ⅜ mile to the Johnson Camp Trail junction. (The mileages given at the junction are correct, not those at Bull Creek.)

Take the right fork south, starting to climb in 200 feet. You will gain 1400 feet in elevation in the 2 miles to Johnson Camp, so the climb is steady and often steep. At first you head southwest, but by ¾ mile your trail climbs southeast. The virgin forest continues almost to the camp, but the redwoods are mostly under 8 feet in diameter, sharing the forest canopy with madrone and Douglas fir.

Your trail levels briefly, then climbs gradually from one mile. At 1¼ miles you can briefly see the steep face of Grasshopper Peak ahead to the south. Continue your steady climb with occasional steep stretches, until the 2-mile point. Then, after a brief downhill stretch, the trail becomes mostly level with a few short climbs. You may hear the sound of running water on your right. At 2¼ miles you bend right and head west to Johnson Camp at 2⅜ miles.

The camp sits south of the trail. Four primitive cabins cluster around a spring at the headwaters of Miller Creek. This shady spot amidst second-growth redwoods housed "tie hacks," men who split redwoods into railroad ties. It was active from about 1920 into the 1950s. Today the facilities include the four cabins, tent sites, a chemical toilet, and a redwood tub for a cool bath on a warm summer day. Mosquitoes thrive in this pleasant spot, so be sure to bring plenty of repellent.

Do not be confused by the maze of old trails and skid roads around the camp. Your trail continues west, descending to

GRASSHOPPER PEAK VIA JOHNSON CAMP:

DISTANCE: 10½ miles round trip from Big Tree.
    13½ via Grasshopper Road (mountain bikes and horses).
    5 miles round trip to Johnson Camp.

TIME: A full day or overnight.

TERRAIN: Through virgin redwood forest, then climbing a ridge to Johnson Camp, then along old road to top of highest peak.

ELEVATION GAIN/LOSS: To Johnson Camp, round trip: 1360 feet+/1360 feet-
    To Grasshopper Peak round trip: 3340 feet+/3340 feet-

BEST TIME: Spring is ideal, but any clear day is good.

WARNINGS: Poison oak grows extensively in Humboldt Redwoods State Park. Long, steep trail. If you are climbing the peak as a day hike, leave early and take water and a lunch. Permit required to camp at Johnson or other backcountry camps.

DIRECTIONS TO TRAILHEAD: Leave Highway 101 at the South Fork/Honeydew exit (M.36.1). Go west on Bull Creek Flats Road. Go 3.8 miles to the Big Tree Road on the left. Mountain bikers and equestrians must use Grasshopper Road on the left at 4.6 miles.

FEES: Johnson Camp and other backcountry camps: $2/night/person.

FURTHER INFO: Humboldt Redwoods State Park (707) 946-2311, 946-2366.

cross a small creek, then contouring to meet Grasshopper Road at 2½ miles. (It is 4.2 miles back to Bull Creek Flats Road if you go right.)

Turn left onto the broad road and climb again. At 2¾ miles you climb steeply, but most of the grade is moderate. You are halfway to the top of Grasshopper Peak (in both miles and elevation). Views open up to the west. Just after 3 miles, you cross another small stream that flows in winter and spring.

At 3⅜ miles your trail turns sharply left and heads northeast. You climb steadily by long switchbacks through young forest. At 3¾ miles you pass a redwood stump at least 16 feet in diameter. This and other giants here were cut 80 to 100 years ago; on some stumps you can see the springboard cuts where the fallers would put planks to stand on.

Between 4⅛ and 4¼ miles, a stand of virgin redwoods is alongside the road, somehow overlooked by the axemen. At 4⅜ the steadily climbing road bends right and heads straight toward the summit.

At 4½ miles you come to the best view yet. Kings Peak (4087 feet) is to the southwest. From here to the summit the soils consist of small, fractured light-color rock, just like the soils of the Kings Crest.

About 5 miles from the trailhead, you meet the turnoff to Grasshopper Camp. Bear left to the camp, right to climb the peak. It is less than ½ mile of level walking to the camp, on the border between forest and meadow. The Grasshopper Trail from Canoe Creek meets the road near the camp. (The bridge across the Eel River on that trail is summer only.) The final ¼ mile to the peak climbs only 160 feet but seems like more. You can see the lookout tower with ⅛ mile to go.

At the top, you are rewarded with a 360-degree view of forest, mountains and sea. To the southwest is Kings Crest with its peaks from right to left: Blue Slide, Shubrick, Kings, Saddle and Horse. South-southwest is a notch where you can see the ocean on a clear day. From southeast to east sit the snowy summits of the Yolla Bollies: Hull, Sanhedrin, flat-topped Black Butte, Anthony, South and North Yolla Bolly, Black Rock and Four Corners Rock, the latter almost due east. South Fork Mountain runs miles north from there. In the foreground are the vast forests of Humboldt Redwoods State Park, the Eel River and Highway 101. To the north-northwest a plume of smoke marks Eureka when it is clear enough. And to the west are several ridges and peaks which extend all the way to Cape Mendocino (beyond view).

If you are on a day hike, be sure to leave enough time to hike the 5¼ miles back to Big Tree or 6¾ miles down Grasshopper Road before dark. Luckily, it is a downhill run.

40.

SQUAW CREEK RIDGE

BACKPACKING BULL CREEK BASIN

Squaw Creek Ridge and the rest of Bull Creek Basin provide varied opportunities for day hikers, backpackers, equestrians and mountain bikers. The shortest route to Squaw Creek Ridge is described below, the first mile open only to hikers. If you want to ride horses or mountain bikes along the ridge, you must start at Grasshopper Road. That route climbs ⅝ mile, then goes to the right on Squaw Creek Ridge Road, climbing ⅝ mile, then for just over one mile to meet the foot trail described below.

To stay at Baxter or Hamilton Barn Environmental Camps or at any of the trail camps, you must first register at the Visitor Center near Burlington Campground.

An old road heads south past bay laurel trees, poison oak, hazel, wild rose and pioneer apple trees, coming to Baxter Camp in ⅛ mile. The camp sits in a redwood grove beside Bull Creek. Just beyond the camp, a sign points left for the trail to Squaw Creek Ridge Road and Whiskey Flat Camp.

The trail climbs steeply, then eases to ¼ mile. Climb steeply again to an old skid trail. You follow the skid, climbing south-southeast. Your trail levels before ⅜ mile, where it bends left and makes a steep, winding ascent through tanoak forest. After ½ mile the climb becomes moderate. You pass a flowering dogwood tree at ¾ mile. Your trail bends left after ⅞ mile and soon comes to Squaw Creek Ridge Road.

Turn right on the wide road, climbing south alongside large redwoods to level at one mile. Stay mostly level to 1¼ miles, then climb gradually to a saddle on the ridge at 1⅜ miles, where big redwoods grow with Douglas firs, tanoaks, madrones, huckleberries and Douglas irises.

Make an easy climb along the ridge to 1⅝ miles, then descend to another saddle. Follow the ridge southwest as ceanothus, wild rose and salal join the understory. After 2 miles you continue along the ridge with short ups and downs.

After a straightaway you start the last big climb to Whiskey Flat Camp. The climb eases at 2¼ miles, then steepens as you bend left in virgin forest. Climb and wind to 2½ miles, then descend into a grove of large redwoods, where rare western yew also grows.

Your road climbs to 2¾ miles where you come to Whiskey Flat Camp. It is a beautiful spot where redwoods of 10-foot diameter tower over salal, redwood sorrel, woodwardia and sword ferns and a babbling brook. A faucet at the camp entrance provides sweet water. The camp was named for a Prohibition-era still located here.

You can use Whiskey Flat Camp as a base for exploring the surrounding wilderness. It is 5½ miles to Grasshopper Peak, an 11-mile round trip with far less elevation change than from the Big Tree Area.

Another option is to use a different trail camp each night. From Whiskey Flat Camp, it is a steady climb to Hanson Ridge Road in 1⅝ miles, 2¼ miles to Hanson Ridge Camp with its wonderful views. From Hanson Ridge Road junction, it is 4 miles via Preacher Gulch Road to Grasshopper Camp, 7 miles to Johnson Camp. Or you can descend steeply southwest on Preacher Gulch Road to Bull Creek Trail Camp, 2 miles from Hanson Ridge Road junction, then follow Bull Creek to the main road. The options are many but you must plan ahead to get the required camping permits. All camps mentioned, except Johnson Camp (hikers only), are accessible to hikers, equestrians and mountain bikers.

SQUAW CREEK RIDGE:

DISTANCE: 5½ miles round trip to Whiskey Flat Camp (Add 1¾ miles each direction from Grasshopper Road).
One way to Hanson Ridge Camp: 5¼ miles
To Grasshopper Camp: 8¼ miles.

TIME: Whiskey Flat can be reached in 1 to 1½ hours. The area is ideal for 1- to 3-night backpack trips.

TERRAIN: Climbing to and traversing ridges. Possible peak climb or descent along stream canyon.

ELEVATION GAIN/LOSS: From Baxter Camp or Grasshopper Road to Whiskey Flat: 1630 feet+/120 feet-
From Whiskey Flat to Hanson Ridge Road junction: 520 feet+/160 feet-
To Hanson Ridge Camp add 240 feet+/100 feet-
From Hanson Ridge junction to Preacher Gulch Road: 160 feet-
To Bull Creek Road and Camp: add 1200 feet-
Preacher Gulch Road to Grasshopper Camp: 1320 feet+/340 feet-
From Grasshopper Camp to peak: add 300 feet+

BEST TIME: Spring and fall. Summer is hot, but Whiskey Flat Camp is always cool.

WARNINGS: Poison oak grows extensively in Humboldt Redwoods State Park. Permit required to camp at Whiskey Flat and other backcountry camps.

DIRECTIONS TO TRAILHEAD: Exit Highway 101 at South Fork/Honeydew exit (M.36.1). Go west on Bull Creek Flats Road. It is 4.6 miles to Grasshopper Road (starting point for horses or mountain bikes), 5.4 miles to Baxter Camp Road. (Environmental Camp and trailhead for hikers only.) Park on the east side of the road where the trail to Baxter Camp heads south.

FEES: Environmental Camps: $6/night. Trail camps: $2/person/night.

FURTHER INFO: Humboldt Redwoods State Park (707) 946-2311, 946-2366.

OTHER SUGGESTION: LOOK PRAIRIE TRAIL (on north, 3.6 miles from highway) climbs to a pioneer barn with a grand view (1⅞ miles round trip). Mountain bikers can make an 11-mile loop by continuing steeply up Look Prairie Road to go left on Peavine Road along the ridge, then descend Thornton Road to Albee Creek.

JOHNSON PRAIRIE TRAIL (on north, 3.9 miles from highway) climbs through prairie to a pioneer grave (1⅝ miles round trip).

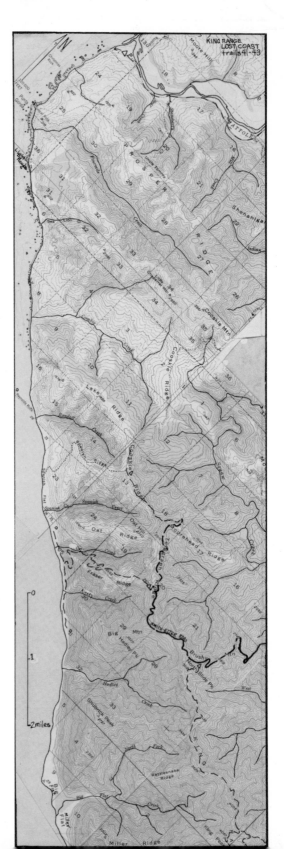

KING RANGE
LOST COAST
trails 41-43

THE LOST COAST

Imagine 25 miles of wilderness beach backed by steep bluffs and cliffs rising to ten peaks over 2000 feet and cut by 15 year-round streams. If you like such wild, rugged country, plan a trip to the Lost Coast.

The King Range is the largest area of wilderness on the Pacific Coast between Olympic National Park and Point Reyes National Seashore. Popularly known as the Lost Coast, the 60,000 acres of King Range National Conservation Area include the wilderness coast, the steep mountains and canyons of the King Range, and the 4000 acres of Chemise Mountain Primitive Area. About 37,000 acres of the King Range are currently being considered for formal wilderness designation. You can get a free map of the area's roads and trails from the Bureau of Land Management office in Arcata or Ukiah.

41.

THE LOST COAST
MATTOLE RIVER SOUTH

Most people enter this wild coast from the north or south end. Though these approaches avoid significant elevation change, the trek is not easy. Walking in strong winds over loose sand and rocks demands hiking boots for backpackers. Three other trailheads reach the middle portion of the Lost Coast, all involving substantial elevation change: Spanish Ridge, Smith-Etter Road and Buck Creek Trail. Consider them for shorter trips or as part of a loop only if you are in good shape.

Of the north and south trailheads, the mouth of the Mattole River on the north provides the most pristine approach. You may be exposed to strong winds for the 3-mile hike to Punta Gorda Lighthouse. Unless you time your hike with the tide as you pass Sea Lion Gulch, you must scramble over crumbling cliffs to stay out of the surf. Walking becomes easier as you pass the deep canyons of Cooskie, Randall and Spanish Creeks.

Prevailing winds blow from northwest to southeast. So the common lore is that you hike the Lost Coast from north to south, with the wind at your back. But unless you intend to go the whole 25 miles, you will likely have the wind against you in one direction or the other.

If you enter from the south via Shelter Cove (see Trail #46), keep in mind that the beach is open to vehicles for the

LOST COAST: MATTOLE RIVER SOUTH:

DISTANCE: 25-mile shuttle, or shorter round trip.

TIME: 3-4 days for entire hike, 4-hour day hike to Punta Gorda Lighthouse.

TERRAIN: Mostly level beach and headland, backed by precipitous cliffs and deep canyons.

BEST TIME: Spring. September and October next best.

WARNINGS: Get a campfire permit at any BLM office or state fire station. Purify water, especially Cooskie Creek north and in Shelter Cove area. Watch for timber rattlers, especially near wood piles. Isolated country with no services. Difficult beach walking in soft sand and over rocks. Two or three points difficult or impassable at high tide.

DIRECTIONS TO TRAILHEAD: Exit Highway 101 at South Fork/Honeydew exit at M.36.1. Go west on Bull Creek Flats Road for 23 miles to Honeydew, then right on Mattole Road for 14 miles to Lighthouse Road, just before Petrolia. Go left on Lighthouse Road to its end at the beach near the mouth of the Mattole River.

FURTHER INFO: Bureau of Land Management, Ukiah (707) 462-3863 or Arcata (707) 822-7648.

first 3 miles, an incongruous intrusion on the solitude of this place. Beyond the vehicle closure lies the most spectacular part of the Lost Coast, a narrow beach backed by high cliffs and steep canyons with lush vegetation and wildflowers.

Wherever you approach the Lost Coast, you will find solitude and physical grandeur to challenge your spirit, and a wondrous diversity of plant and animal life growing right to the ocean's edge. Be careful, watch for rogue waves, and treat the wilderness with respect.

From the end of Lighthouse Road you head south along the broad, dark sand beach. The firm sand just above the tide line provides the best walking, except where a firmly packed jeep trail follows the base of the bluffs. Sheep graze the steep grasslands on your left.

Before one mile the first of many year-round creeks cascades down the steep, grassy bluff. The beach gets rockier to the south. Tide pools and sea stacks lie offshore. After 1½ miles the broad beach narrows. Beyond a small point, several seasonal streams drop to the beach.

At 2½ miles an old ranch road winds steeply up the bluff. You immediately round Punta Gorda as the lighthouse comes into view. From here you can walk on a firm roadbed. You pass two cabins near Fourmile Creek at 2⅝ miles. After the ford, continue on a firm track across the grassy bluff, passing more dilapidated ranch buildings.

At 3 miles a path forks left to Punta Gorda Lighthouse ruin. The light station helped ships navigate this fogbound, rugged coast from 1911 to 1951. It was built after the wreck of the *SS Columbia* claimed 87 lives here in 1907. Today only the squat light tower remains, the keeper's quarters and fog signal house having been razed by BLM in 1970. The wind usually roars and whistles through the concrete tower.

You cross several small creeks in the next ½ mile as you follow the old jeep road along the coast. After the creek at 3½ miles, you climb a hill to stay on the road, or you can return to the beach. On the road you have another chance to return to the beach at 3¾ miles. Either way, you come to steep Sea Lion Gulch at 4 miles. Sea Lion Rocks lie just offshore, home to three dozen Steller sea lions and many cormorants and pelicans. The steep mouth of the creek provides shelter from the wind, views of the sea lions and wildflowers.

The beach narrows after the gulch. At 4½ miles beach passage may be blocked at high tide. If necessary, you can scramble over crumbling rock and mud slides, on a steep, rough detour above the surf. You might consider waiting for the tide to drop below +5.0 feet, when the beach is passable. When the tide is out, uneven-sized rocks on the beach slow your progress.

You pass a barn and cabin above the beach at 4¾ miles. Then walking becomes easier at the base of steep cliffs. At 6 miles you come to the broad, deep canyon of Cooskie Creek. A sweat lodge of driftwood sits beside its mouth. Sheltered camps lie within ¼ mile upstream. Fishing is fair for trout to 9 inches. You should purify drinking water. Private property lies about one mile upstream.

Continuing southeast, you must boulder-hop for a few hundred feet. Then footing improves as the beach widens. You pass small waterfalls and two narrow spots to 7 miles. From 7¼ to 7¾ miles, the cliffs above the beach have massive landslides. At 7½ miles large, uneven rocks on a steeply slanting beach make rough walking. The bluffs, however, are worse, cut by many little canyons. After 7¾ miles loose sand and gravel slow progress.

About 8 miles from the trailhead, Reynolds Rock lies offshore. You pass a point showing greatly twisted rock strata. The geological folding continues to the mouth of Randall Creek at 8⅝ miles.

Narrower and more wooded than Cooskie Creek, Randall Creek also provides fair fishing. A pleasant camp lies a short walk upstream on the north side of the creek.

A road along the bluffs south of the creek provides firm footing. Just 250 feet from Randall Creek, the Spanish Ridge Trail meets your road. Then your path climbs the rolling grassland at the base of the steep bluffs. At 8⅞ miles you cross a small stream where watercress grows. Offshore rocks line this stretch of coast. Near 9¾ miles a mostly level footpath crosses the lower bluff. Or you can walk the old road, which leads up and down along the upper bluff. You pass two more streams jammed with wildflowers, the second with watercress and mint.

At 10¼ miles the grassy headlands get broader and flatter as you come to the north end of Spanish Flat. If it is not too windy these lush grasslands provide good camping. At 10½ miles another spur climbs Spanish Ridge. You walk the broad grassy flat, once the site of a sawmill. The lumber was hauled to market by ship. Wildflowers lie scattered through the grasslands. Woodwardia ferns grow at the base of the steep bluffs.

At 11⅜ miles you come to the broad flood plain of deep Spanish Creek Canyon. Several campsites lie in or near the canyon. In ¼ mile you pass an elk wallow in the road. You might spot these large animals in the surrounding grasslands. You pass an old corral, then come to pioneer Paul Smith's cabin, 12 miles from the trailhead. It overlooks a broad sandy beach.

At 12⅜ miles you cross Oat Creek. The creek cascades down its twisting, rocky gorge. Swallows dip and soar overhead. Mimulus, iris, sticky monkeyflower, columbine, yarrow, paintbrush, cow parsnip, penstemon and lupine grow in the sheltered canyon. You meet the Smith-Etter Road at 13 miles (see Trail #42).

The road continues southeast along the coast, crossing the broad, gravelly wash of Kinsey Creek in ¼ mile. It leads along grasslands below steep bluffs, passing the Etter cabin at 14 miles. The headlands narrow as a sandy track heads for Hadley Creek (also known as Big Creek), which you cross at 14⅝ miles. Dense forest grows in the deep, shady canyon.

Your trail continues in loose sand along a narrow beach. At 14⅞ miles the beach is backed by high sand dunes stacked against a steep grassy hill. A trail climbs the steep headlands to the south. It provides better walking than continued slogging in the sand. At 15 miles the faint double track is obliterated by a slide, but a narrow trail continues. Back on the grasslands the trail becomes vague; stay high on the headlands below steep bluffs. You cross a stream choked with watercress at 15⅛ miles. Then your trail descends to meet a gently rolling grassland, soon returning to an obvious dirt road.

You cross a small creek at 15¾ miles and come to Big Flat, which stretches along the coast for over a mile. The first of many Indian shell middens lies beside the road. It is unlawful to disturb these archaeological sites. The road provides easy walking for your sand- and rock-weary soles. As Big Flat broadens to its widest point, the road draws away from the shore. At 16¼ miles your path crosses a landing strip used by the residents of the house ahead.

As you approach the canyon of Big Flat Creek, watch for the small timber rattlesnakes that live on the flat and in the rocky wash of the creek. Other animals frequenting Big Flat include Roosevelt elk, deer, fox, badger, rubber boa snake (harmless) and various lizards. Douglas firs and cypresses grow along the edge of the flat.

After paralleling the runway, your trail forks. The roadbed continues along the runway, then heads into the canyon, where the most protected campsites lie among trees alongside the broad, gravelly wash. If you are continuing south or want to camp at Miller Flat, take the trail that forks right, crosses the runway, and follows the edge of the alder and willow forest near the beach. It passes two camps around 16¾ miles. The second one has a driftwood shelter tall

149

enough to stand up in, with a nifty flag. From here you can look up Big Flat Creek Canyon to 4087-foot Kings Peak. Then you cross Big Flat Creek. Stay right of the trees on the far side. Watch for rattlers!

You come to Miller Flat, broader and more wooded than Big Flat. Wild rose, chemise, gooseberry, red alder and poison oak grow near the creek. Several campsites lie near the trail. More sheltered camps are in the forest to the northeast. Your trail turns east, climbing gradually up the broad flat, a favorite browse for deer. Easy walking across Miller Flat brings you to 17⅝ miles, where a short descent drops you back on the beach at 17¾ miles.

You again walk the beach at the base of steep bluffs. On your right lie many offshore rocks and tide pools. After a small, unmapped creek, the beach becomes very rocky. You round a small point at 18⅜ miles as the beach gets narrower.

Ahead lies another stretch where progress may be blocked at a tide of +4.5 feet or more. The rugged cliffs above have many small creeks, seeps and springs, supporting hanging gardens of wildflowers in spring and early summer. The narrowest point lies just before Shipman Creek at 18¾ miles.

Beautiful Shipman Creek has camps in the driftwood on either side of its mouth. The deep wooded canyon is a treat to explore. At low tide you can visit the rewarding tide pools west of its mouth. You are 6¼ miles from Shelter Cove.

You walk a broad beach until 19½ miles, where you cross a small creek. You round a point as the beach turns rocky and narrow. Pass Buck Creek at 20 miles and meet the Buck Creek Trail, which climbs 3300 feet in the 2½ miles to Saddle Mountain Road.

Many more creeks tumble down the cliffs on your way to Gitchell Creek at 21½ miles. A campsite sits beside its mouth. But the vehicle users allowed this far north on the beach from Shelter Cove have degraded the place with trash.

After another mile of sandy beach, you can follow a dirt road along the bluffs. At 23½ miles is the mouth of wooded Horse Mountain Creek, where the road returns to the beach. Big rocks lie along the beach at 23⅞ miles, before another steep creek. The beach broadens as you turn south, heading straight for Point Delgada. As you walk the beach or bluff road along the base of the rugged Kaluna Cliff, your thoughts may turn to the cold beer or ice cream available in Shelter Cove. You cross Telegraph Creek at 25 miles and come to the parking area.

42

SMITH-ETTER ROAD TO BEACH

STEEP SHORTCUT TO HEART OF LOST COAST

This is the shortest hiking route into the heart of the Lost Coast. Although it entails a longer drive on dirt roads to get to this trailhead, the extra effort by car allows you to hike just 4 miles to reach the middle section of the Lost Coast, 12 miles from the north and south trailheads. Remember that you must climb 2400 feet in elevation to return to your car from the beach.

The Smith-Etter Road was reopened to vehicle traffic in spring, 1987. Currently the Bureau of Land Management is considering reopening the road to within ¼ mile of the beach. It would be unfortunate to make access to the center portion of the Lost Coast so easy for vehicle traffic. The Wilderness Society and the California Wilderness Coalition are lobbying against further opening of the road. The final decision will not come until at least 1991, when Congress will examine the various proposals for wilderness status for the King Range and make the final decision. In the meantime, you can drive 8 steep, winding miles on the Smith-Etter Road, park at the locked gate and hike to the beach.

The locked gate blocks Smith-Etter Road at its junction with the Telegraph Ridge Road. Park near the gate, being sure not to block traffic on Telegraph Ridge Road (which you can drive northwest for 1½ miles to the Spanish Ridge Trail).

Behind the gate your route follows the Smith-Etter Road northwest, then west, below the summit of Telegraph Ridge. On your left the steep drainage of Kinsey Creek drops to the ocean far below. The trail climbs slightly for ½ mile. After ¼ mile, big Douglas firs grow where a little gully crosses the road. This pleasantly sheltered spot has room to camp on flat ground on either side of the road. When the wind dies down you can hear the roar of the surf.

At ½ mile your climb levels atop Kinsey Ridge which you follow to the beach. A wide spot on the ridge marks ¾ mile. The trail descends steadily from there. The low, brushy vegetation allows views northwest into deep Oat Creek Canyon and grassy Oat Ridge and Spanish Ridge beyond.

At one mile you have another view of the beach at the mouth of Kinsey Creek. Then you leave the ridgetop, bending right to descend along its north face. After 1½ miles you regain the top of the ridge as its descends steeply toward the shore. Wildflowers along the road include bush lupine, wild rose, sticky monkeyflower, Douglas iris, morning glory, thistle and pennyroyal.

The road starts a series of long switchbacks at 1¾ miles. These descend into a dark forest of Douglas fir and live oak. Return to the ridge briefly at 2¼ miles, then switch right to its north side. Many birds frequent this area. Poppy, coastal manroot and poison oak grow on the road shoulders.

At 3 miles you come to the westernmost bend in the road, high above the mouth of Oat Creek. You switch sharply left here and descend steeply southeast. The wilderness coast stretches magnificently before you. The broad shoal of Big Flat lies 4 miles away. Far beyond it Point Delgada extends into the Pacific. You can see the Etter cabin to the south and Paul Smith's cabin not far to the north. The point where the road comes to the beach is also visible, still 800 feet below.

At 3¼ miles you switchback right and descend by five more steep switchbacks to the beach, 3¾ miles from the locked gate. Sticky monkeyflower, rattlesnake grass and beach morning glory grow at the junction. A sign proclaims that it is 4¾ miles back up the road to the Kings Crest Trail,

---

SMITH-ETTER ROAD TO BEACH:

DISTANCE: One way: 3¾ miles.

TIME: 2-3 hours each way.

TERRAIN: Road walking down Kinsey Ridge to the beach. Steep climb back.

ELEVATION GAIN/LOSS: 140 feet+/2460 feet- one way

BEST TIME: Spring or fall.

WARNINGS: Road closed in wet weather, usually November to March; inquire. Unmaintained road requires high clearance vehicle, may require four-wheel drive. See also warnings for Trail #41.

DIRECTIONS TO TRAILHEAD: Follow directions in Trail #41 to Honeydew. Then go left for 2 miles, then right on Landergren Road, which becomes Smith-Etter Road after the gate. Drive 8 steep, rough and winding miles to trailhead.

FURTHER INFO: Bureau of Land Management (707) 822-7648, Arcata or (707) 462-3863, Ukiah.

OTHER SUGGESTION: SPANISH RIDGE TRAIL starts from Telegraph Ridge Road, off Smith-Etter Road, descending 2000 feet in 3 miles to Spanish Flat.

---

but the actual distance is 6⅛ miles.

From the junction a road runs south to Kinsey Creek in just ¼ mile. Big Flat is 4½ miles, while the southern trailhead at Shelter Cove lies 12 miles to the southeast.

Along the coast to the north, Paul Smith's cabin lies at the foot of Oat Ridge in one mile. Spanish Flat is 1¾ miles away. It is 10 miles to the Punta Gorda Lighthouse, 13 miles to the northern trailhead at the mouth of the Mattole River. See Trails #41 and 46 for more details on the Lost Coast.

43.

KINGS CREST NORTH

SMITH-ETTER ROAD TO KINGS PEAK

The Kings Crest Trail traverses the high ridge of King Range National Conservation Area. One of the more rugged hikes in the area, Kings Crest Trail provides spectacular views of the wilderness coast to the west. The trail offers developed campsites at Miller and Maple Camps and other more primitive camp choices. After 5½ miles the trail reaches the 4087-foot summit of Kings Peak, where the views are unsurpassed. The trail is ideal for a backpack trip of one or two nights. It can also be done as a long, rather rigorous day hike of 11 miles. More often than not you will have the trail to yourself. Carry water since there is none along the main trail, and the sources at Miller and Maple Camp may dry up by summer. The Smith-Etter Road may be closed in wet weather, limiting access to the trailhead.

The trail starts by climbing an old jeep road through dense brush. You soon come to a flat clearing with views east. The trail then descends along the east face of North Slide Peak with fine views of the rugged ridge you follow southeast to

DISTANCE: 5½ miles one way, 11 miles round trip.

TIME: Best as an overnight, though possible as long day hike.

TERRAIN: Up and down along a rugged ridge to reach the top of Kings Peak.

ELEVATION GAIN/LOSS: 2210 feet+/1380 feet-, one way. 3590 feet+/3590 feet-, round trip.

BEST TIME: Spring is best. Summer or fall also good.

WARNINGS: Isolated country, no services. Watch for timber rattlers. May be snow on trail in winter or early spring. Road to trail may be closed in rainy season.

DIRECTIONS TO TRAILHEAD: Follow directions for Trail #42, except that you come to the trailhead after 6 miles on the Smith-Etter Road.

FURTHER INFO: Bureau of Land Management, Arcata (707) 822-7648 or Ukiah (707) 462-3873.

Kings Peak. Your trail descends an open, brushy slope to ½ mile, then descends gradually along a shaded section.

At ⅞ mile make a big bend left and cross another barren stretch to the end of the old jeep track at one mile. A broad spot on the trail sits in a saddle of the ridge, a level spot for a dry camp. The trail turns east, climbing steadily for ⅛ mile to a summit where one-leaved wild onion grows.

Make a short, steep descent to 1¼ miles. Then your trail levels for nearly ¼ mile before climbing steeply again along the razor ridge. More than a dozen steep, short switchbacks wind up the north side of the ridge. Meet the Miller Camp Trail at 1¾ miles, which forks left and descends 800 feet in 2 miles to the camp, which has a spring.

After the junction, your trail turns south and descends, soon returning to the ridge. Two miles from the trailhead, you come to a saddle with great views along the razor ridge and west into Hadley Creek Canyon. In spring wildflowers sprinkle the steep slide below you. To the south you can see the old (not maintained) Shubrick Peak Trail approaching the summit.

Your trail climbs gradually to meet the Shubrick Peak Trail on the right in ⅜ mile. (It is overgrown but passable.) In 300 feet the south end of the Miller Camp Trail rises to meet your trail on the left (one mile to Miller Camp).

Now your trail climbs by five switchbacks to another top at

2⅝ miles. Then make a shady descent, followed by a short uphill to 2⅞ miles, where a shady campsite sits in the middle of the trail. Descending to the 3-mile point, you meet the Rattlesnake Ridge Trail. The side trail is easy to miss, however. It sits on a relatively flat section of trail. Only a fragment of an old wooden trail sign marks the junction. The unmaintained trail heads south, descending to a campsite and a possible water source (many people search, few find it).

The Kings Crest Trail now climbs the ridge by several switchbacks to a summit of 3620 feet. Then you descend steeply to a brushy area along the ridge at 3¼ miles. You follow the ridge up, down, up and down again in the next stretch with frequent views of Big Flat Creek and the blue Pacific 3000 feet below.

From 3¾ miles you climb steeply again. At 4 miles the trail becomes easier, staying relatively level through a pleasantly shaded forest of Douglas fir, although you cross steep slopes which are prone to slides. At 4½ miles a clearing provides views of the Mattole Valley and the Yolla Bolly and Trinity Mountains.

Then your trail descends gradually to a saddle with breathtaking views of the steep and rugged country on both sides of the ridge. The headwaters of Big Flat Creek lie just ¼ mile to the south and 1000 feet below. Your trail climbs a bit, then crosses two large rock fields at 4¾ miles. You descend through fir and hardwood forests along a steep slope, then climb briefly to reach the junction with the Lightning Trail, 5 miles from your trailhead. The left fork leads to Maple Camp in ⅝ mile, Lightning Trailhead in 2 miles. You take the right fork and climb 600 feet in ½ mile to the top of Kings Peak. See Trail #45 for a detailed description of the fantastic view from the summit.

44.

LIGHTNING TRAIL TO KINGS PEAK
STEEP BUT SHADY ROUTE

The Lightning Trail requires the shortest drive of the three trailheads to Kings Peak. It is the most accessible in winter, although the King Range Road may also be closed by slides in the rainy season. This route has two other advantages: it is the shadiest route, ideal in hot weather; it has the best access to both water and campsites. Although the Lightning Trail has more of a climb than the ridge route, it is well graded and pleasant.

The Lightning Trail starts on a high bank on the left side of

DISTANCE: 2½ miles to summit, 5 miles round trip.

TIME: At least 2½ hours to top and back.

TERRAIN: A brush-and-forest-covered ridge leading to the summit of Kings Peak.

ELEVATION GAIN/LOSS: 2000 feet+/-, round trip.

BEST TIME: The best year-round trail to the peak, still nicest in spring.

WARNINGS: Timber rattlers and ticks live in the area; watch for them. Isolated country with no services. Best to carry water in the dry season when water sources are not reliable.

DIRECTIONS TO TRAILHEAD: FROM THE NORTH: Leave Highway 101 at the South Fork/Honeydew exit, M.36.1. Follow Mattole Road west for 23 miles to Honeydew and the junction with the Wilder Ridge Road. Turn left on the latter and go 5 miles to the junction with Horse Mountain Road. Turn right and go 3 miles on steep, winding Horse Mountain Road to the junction with King Range Road. Take a sharp right and go 6.3 miles to the Lightning Trailhead.

FROM THE SOUTH: Leave Highway 101 at Garberville (M.11.4). Take Briceland Road from Redway (2.8 miles north of Garberville on old Highway 101). Go 18 miles and turn right onto unpaved Kings Crest Road. Follow this for 9.5 miles, going left at the junction with Horse Mountain Road. It is 6.3 miles from the junction to the trailhead.

FURTHER INFO: Bureau of Land Management, Ukiah (707) 462-3873 or Arcata (707) 822-7648.

King Range Road, just beyond a big curve left and a wide spot where you can park. The trail heads southeast, coming to a garbage can and a trail register in 100 feet. Sign in, please. The trail climbs through a mixed hardwood forest of madrone, tanoak and huckleberry.

You soon switch left and head east where the trail is a bit vague. The trail steepens and climbs moderately through a series of lazy switchbacks. Just beyond ⅛ mile you pass through a sunny clearing surrounded by manzanita.

The trail climbs steadily along a hardwood-covered ridge. At ¼ mile you pass an old Douglas fir and bend to the left. The trail runs southeast, then south, climbing the ridge with occasional switchbacks.

By ½ mile a steep drop lies on the right. Continue your climb, meandering in and out of virgin Douglas fir forest as you approach the sound of a stream. After ⅝ mile, a right fork leads to pretty Big Rock Camp, beside a stream with big, moss-covered rocks and Douglas firs of 8 feet in diameter.

Climb steeply by many switchbacks for the next ¼ mile. At ⅞ mile you switch left and head southeast onto the relatively cool and wooded north side of the ridge. You regain the top of the ridge briefly at one mile before you climb west through the forest.

After a straight, uphill stretch, you switch left at 1⅛ miles. A spring of delicious water flows from the base of a tree above the bend; it may dry up in summer or fall. Salal and Oregon grape cover the forest floor.

You soon return to the dry ridge, where manzanita and canyon live oak mix with the fir forest. Climb the ridge, passing through a thicket of spiny whitethorn ceanothus, which has fragrant white flowers in May. At 1⅜ miles you climb through a dense forest of young Douglas fir.

Just 1⅝ miles from the trailhead, you come to a junction. The left fork leads to Maple Camp in ¼ mile (shady camp by a stream) and to Saddle Mountain Trailhead in 3 miles. Take the right fork northwest. It is one mile to the top of Kings Peak, 5 miles to the Smith-Etter Road.

The trail continues to climb through forest and brush fields to meet the main trail at 2 miles. Make a sharp left for the top of Kings Peak. The trail gets brushy here; it may be scratchy on bare legs and arms. You climb by switchbacks, then follow a brushy ridge to 2¼ miles, where you go right on the trail to the summit.

Climb a jagged ridge, with views down the west face of the peak to Big Flat and the ocean far below. Indian warriors brighten the way in spring with their bold, dark red flowers. Reach the summit less than ¼ mile from the turnoff. See Trail #45 for a description of the view on a clear day.

From the peak you can return to the Lightning Trailhead in about one hour.

45.

KINGS CREST SOUTH
SADDLE MOUNTAIN TO THE TOP OF THE WORLD

From the end of Saddle Mountain Road, the Kings Crest Trail follows the high ridge of the King Range to the top of Kings Peak. At 4087 feet, the peak is the highest point along the entire California coast. Brush fields alternate with fir forests in this steep, rugged country. This route to the peak is

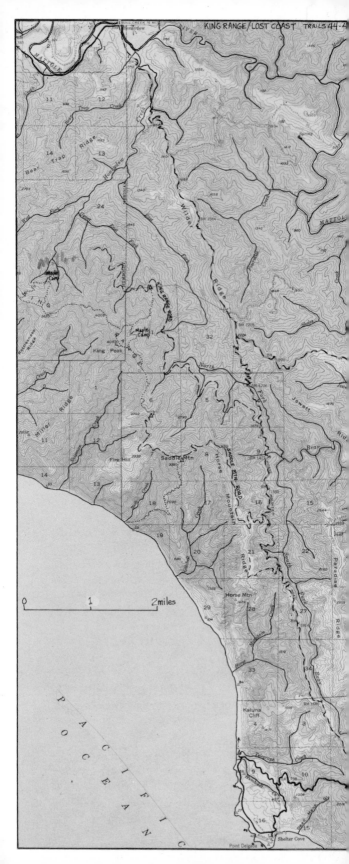

a pleasant, moderate day hike, climaxing in spectacular views. But be sure to read the "directions to trailhead" to prepare you for the drive to the starting point.

The Legend of Kings Peak claims that a Manila galleon was wrecked on the Lost Coast. Survivors or Indians carried away its gold, jewels and spices to a cave and hid them. Years later an earthquake sealed the cave and obliterated all traces of it. My own favorite treasure is the view from the top.

The trail heads north from the parking area, passing a trail register in 300 feet. For the first ¼ mile, you descend through mixed forest of Douglas fir, sugar pine and hardwoods. Bear grass and spiky Oregon grape grow in the understory. The trail levels for ⅛ mile, then descends through forest of madrone, tanoak, canyon live oak and scattered fir.

At ½ mile you can see the glimmer of the ocean through the trees on your left. To the north lie the steep slopes of Kings Peak, scarred by a massive landslide. At ⅝ mile the trail starts to climb. Soon a gnarled, gravity-defying canyon live oak on the left affords views of the sheer drop to the headwaters of Shipman Creek.

Now the climb starts in earnest, making ten switchbacks through manzanita, madrone and oak. At one mile a clearing provides the best views yet to the east and south.

For another ⅛ mile, you climb through manzanita brush fields (can be unpleasant on a warm day). Then your climb eases as the trail plunges into cool mixed forest. At 1⅜ miles the trail levels on a brushy ridge. Views open up to the ocean far below and Kings Peak to the northwest.

Your trail returns to the east side of the ridge and climbs north. At 1½ miles you can see Wilder Ridge below you, dotted with houses and barns. The Mattole River Canyon lies beyond the ridge. Beyond that, the parallel ridges of the Coast Range stretch to the horizon.

Your climb steepens at 1⅝ miles. You switchback twice and regain the brushy ridge top. After 1¾ miles you reach cabin-sized boulders on each side of the trail. The Trinity Alps may be visible to the northeast beyond the very long and straight South Fork Mountain. Just up the trail you have views down the ocean side of the ridge. Make a steep, winding climb for ⅛ mile to reach a broad flat covered with low manzanita.

At 2 miles a steel sign marks the junction. The right fork descends to Maple Camp (½ mile), a possible water source, and to Lightning Trailhead (2½ miles, 1000 feet below). Take the left fork. This leads to another junction at 2⅛ miles. Go left here to reach the summit. (The right fork continues

northwest, eventually coming to the ocean. Even if that is your destination, the detour to the top of Kings Peak is worth the trip.) From the junction you can see the simple shelter on the east face of Kings Peak. The summit lies a brisk ¼ mile up the trail, 200 feet more in elevation. Suddenly you come out on top of the world.

The top consists of a 30-feet-by-40-feet semi-flat area, dropping off steeply on all sides. To the west the ocean glimmers in sunlight. Infinite waves roll toward the shore, reflecting light and heat over chilly ocean depths. Purplish streaks far offshore mark the deepest water, beyond which a snow-white fog bank often obscures the horizon.

The rugged King Range stretches northwest, ending just beyond view at Cape Mendocino, westernmost point of the continental United States. To the northeast lie the Trinity Mountains. The jagged Trinity Alps rise to 8000 feet beyond the lower Trinities. On the clearest of days you can see the round bulk of Lassen Peak (10,487 feet) to the east-northeast, 141 miles away. Directly to the east, at half the distance, the 6000-foot peaks of the Yolla Bollies show in sharp relief.

As you look south down the coast, Saddle Mountain looms in the foreground. Shelter Cove juts seaward to its right. South of Shelter Cove fall (in order) Chemise Mountain, Mistake Point, Cape Vizcaino, Bruhel Point, then the white sands of Ten Mile Dunes. The sawmill smokestack marking Fort Bragg may be seen to the right of the dunes.

Take a moment to reflect on the geology of this place. Directly west of Kings Peak is Big Flat, 4000 feet below (just 3 miles as the crow flies). The San Andreas fault lies just offshore. Over eons, as the onshore tectonic plate moves south, it collides with the Pacific plate moving north. This immense and powerful collision has uplifted these rugged mountains.

KINGS CREST SOUTH:

DISTANCE: 4¾ miles round trip, or 6 miles with semi-loop.

TIME: Plan at least 3 hours hiking time.

TERRAIN: A high, rugged coastal ridge leading to the summit of steep and brushy Kings Peak.

ELEVATION GAIN/LOSS: 1280 feet+/320 feet-, one way
1600 feet+/1600 feet-, round trip

BEST TIME: Clear weather. Spring is best; September and October next best.

WARNINGS: Isolated country without services. Last 7 miles of road are steep and rough, prone to washouts in winter. No water available on trail. Watch for ticks and timber rattlesnakes. May be snow on trail in winter, early spring.

DIRECTIONS TO TRAILHEAD: Leave Highway 101 at Garberville (M.11.4) from the south or Redway (M.14.6) from the north. Take Briceland Road west from Redway for 18 miles (steep and winding, but paved). Go right on unpaved Kings Crest Road for 7 miles. Then turn left on Saddle Mountain Road, marked "Kings Crest Trail." The driving gets rough here. (While most cars can make it to the trailhead, consider Lightning Trailhead as the "better road" alternative if your car has low clearance, a weak transmission or bad tires, or if you visit in winter. If you take the high road, drive slowly and alertly as it is steep, winding and poorly maintained. In one mile you top Horse Mountain Ridge. Go right, coming to Buck Creek Trailhead at 4.5 miles (see other suggestion). At 7 miles you reach the end of the road and Kings Crest Trailhead.

FURTHER INFO: Bureau of Land Management (707) 462-3873, Ukiah or (707) 822-7648, Arcata.

OTHER SUGGESTION: BUCK CREEK TRAIL leaves from 4.5 miles up the Saddle Mountain Road. It descends 3300 feet to the beach at the mouth of Buck Creek in just 2½ miles. It is the shortest and steepest route to the beach from Kings Crest. Not recommended for a stroll to and from the beach. Experienced backpackers may choose to make a 27-mile Crest to Coast Loop: descend to beach at Buck Creek, head north for 9 miles, where you climb east on the Smith-Etter Road for 6 miles. Then take Kings Crest Trail for 7½ miles to return to Saddle Mountain Road. Follow the road for 2½ miles to your starting point. Trails #41, 42, 43 and 45 provide further detail. You can do it in the opposite direction, but the climb from the beach to Saddle Mountain may conjure thoughts of an eternity in hell.

From here it takes about an hour to return to Saddle Mountain Trailhead. You can add 1¼ miles by the following short loop. From east of the shelter, take the trail descending north. It rejoins the main trail in ¼ mile. You follow a brushy ridge east for nearly ¼ mile, then descend by switchbacks to meet the Maple Camp Trail at ⅝ mile. Turn right toward Maple Camp, descending to meet the Lightning Trail (⅞ mile from the peak, 1⅝ miles to Lightning Trailhead). One-quarter mile farther is Maple Camp in the shady canyon by a creek that roars in winter and spring.

From Maple Camp the return trail heads upstream, fords the creek at 1¼ miles, and climbs to meet the main trail at 1¾ miles. You are 2 miles from the Saddle Mountain Trailhead.

46.

SHELTER COVE NORTH

LOST COAST, SOUTH END

The subdivision of Shelter Cove sprawls over the steep, grassy bluffs of Point Delgada. It sits like a mirage, surrounded by the rugged wilderness peaks and canyons of the King Range. In the northwest corner of the subdivision, Beach Road ends at Black Sands Beach, the southern trailhead for the 25 miles of wilderness beach called the Lost Coast. If you have forgotten anything, Shelter Cove has two small general merchandise stores.

The first 3½ miles of beach are open to motorized vehicles, a sad commentary on the Bureau of Land Management's policy for this pristine wilderness. Still, on a typical weekday, hikers may find little or no motorized traffic. The whining engines of the vehicles are less of an intrusion than the trash discarded by some of the riders. This trailhead allows you to reach some of the most spectacular areas of the Lost Coast in an overnight hike. The virgin canyon of Shipman Creek lies just 6¼ miles from the trailhead. Miller Flat and Big Flat are about 2 miles farther.

You walk north on the broad beach, quickly crossing Telegraph Creek. At ⅛ mile a hard-packed road on the bluffs parallels the beach. It climbs a short, steep hill sprinkled with wildflowers and soon descends to a campsite at the top of the beach at ⅜ mile. Although the road climbs the bluff again, it soon ends at a rough crossing of the creek that comes off the steep face of Kaluna Cliff. Hike the broad beach north, crossing another creek at 1⅛ miles, beyond which big rocks stand on the beach.

At 1½ miles you come to Horse Mountain Creek, a deep wooded canyon with a mouth bracketed by steep, grassy slopes. The beach tapers to its narrowest point at 1¾ miles, then broadens. Before 2 miles a primitive road runs along the bluffs again, near a private house. You can follow the bluff road for ½ mile, as the coast bends northwest. A washout near 2½ miles forces you to return to the beach.

The broad beach narrows ⅝ mile beyond Gitchell Creek. You continue along the base of steep cliffs with many cascading streams. At 4⅝ miles the beach tapers to a point that may be impassable at very high tide. You continue along the narrow, rocky beach to Buck Creek at 5⅛ miles. The Buck Creek Trail climbs east from the south side of the creek.

Continuing along the beach, you quickly come to another rocky, narrow section of beach. It should be passable at all but the highest tide. The narrow beach continues past many offshore rocks. The high cliffs on your right have many springs and hanging gardens of wildflowers.

At 5½ miles a creek cascades to the beach, just short of a rocky promontory. It plunges 1600 feet in its short, ¾-mile course. Offshore lies the deep submarine trench of Delgada Canyon, which is 450 feet deep just ½ mile from shore. Beyond the rocky point, the beach becomes very broad.

You come to Shipman Creek 6¼ miles from the trailhead. Huge piles of driftwood lie in the protected mouth of the wooded canyon, which has camps on both sides. Clear pools and waterfalls lie upstream, while wildflowers thrive on the grassy bluff east of its mouth.

To continue along the beach, you need a tide lower than +4.5 feet. The narrow beach is backed by 10-foot cliffs topped by steep, grassy bluffs. Beyond 6⅝ miles the beach gets wider, though steep cliffs still tower overhead. At 7¼ miles a

DISTANCE: Up to 25 miles.
TIME: 1 or more days.
TERRAIN: Level beach walking.
BEST TIME: Spring or fall.
WARNINGS: Watch for timber rattlers and vehicles on beach.
DIRECTIONS TO TRAILHEAD: Follow directions west from Redway. As you descend to Shelter Cove, take first right—Ridge Road.
FURTHER INFO: Bureau of Land Management (707) 462-3873, Ukiah; (707) 822-7648, Arcata.

painted rock covered with iceplant marks a path that climbs onto rolling and grassy Miller Flat. You come to Big Flat Creek at 8 miles. The base of the Smith-Etter Road lies 4 miles beyond. For more details of this area and the north end of the Lost Coast, see Trail #41.

≠47.

HIDDEN VALLEY TO CHEMISE MOUNTAIN TO WHALE GULCH

Much of this old pack trail has recently been reconstructed. It connects the northern and southern sections of the Lost Coast Trail. You can now start backpacking at the mouth of the Mattole River, walk 25 miles along the beach to Shelter Cove, then hike or hitchhike 3 miles of paved road to Hidden Valley Trailhead. From there it is a 28-mile hike to the Usal Trailhead, 6 miles north of Highway 1. The 4½ miles south from Hidden Valley Trailhead provide excellent walking. But the next 2½ miles, descending the ridge to the mouth of Whale Gulch, are steep and brushy. The trail was poorly marked and not yet reconstructed at press time. A property dispute may restrict access to this portion of the trail; inquire.

Walk past the gate heading southwest on an old road. Young Douglas fir mix with alder, bay laurel, hazel, and thimble-berry. Wild mint grows in the middle of the road. You will notice the harsh devastation of a forest fire on the left. This hike winds in and out of the area burned by the Chemise Mountain fire of 1973.

At ⅛ mile the road swings left and crosses a tiny, slow-flowing creek. In spring the purple shades of bush lupine, Douglas iris, and ceanothus brighten the path.

You quickly come to a lush green meadow stretching for ½ mile up a valley surrounded by chaparral and fire-scarred forest. A tall fence running along its northern boundary keeps elk from wandering north when they are relocated here from Prairie Creek Redwoods State Park. Poppies and lupine sprinkle the heavenly meadow of Hidden Valley in the spring. Views of the blue Pacific lie to the west and south. In the upper end of the valley, an apple orchard marks the site of an old ranch.

At ¼ mile your road forks. You take the left fork; the right fork continues into Hidden Valley. You climb moderately, with views of the valley and the ocean beyond. Before ½ mile you come to the upper end of the apple orchard. Your trail switches left and heads north, climbing steeply away from the road. As you climb by several steep, short switchbacks, you are rewarded with views of Hidden Valley.

You climb into unburned forest, then descend briefly back into the burn. The climb resumes, entering hardwood forest at ¾ mile. It changes to fir forest by ⅞ mile. Then your steep climb winds to gain the ridge at one mile.

The ridge soon becomes brushy. You descend the ridge to 1¼ miles, where you return to forest. Climb briefly, only to descend again, with ceanothus along the trail. Your trail levels at 1⅜ miles, then makes a steep, short climb to 1½ miles. Another level stretch leads to another short climb.

You climb steeply to 1¾ miles, then level at the junction with the trail from Wailaki and Nadelos Campgrounds. Turn right for Chemise Mountain and Whale Gulch. You climb gradually, heading south just below the ridgetop.

About 2 miles from the trailhead, your trail levels. The high peaks of the Yolla Bolly Mountains appear to the east. You climb atop the ridge at 2⅛ miles, but tall brush conceals the views. You continue level or climbing gently along the ridge. At 2¼ miles the chaparral parts to reveal a view of Shelter Cove to the northwest.

In less than ¼ mile, your climb brings you to a sign marking the 2598-foot summit of Chemise Mountain on your left. A narrow, overgrown trail winds to the very top in about 150 feet. The side trip is worthwhile because the brush opens to present fine vistas in all directions. Immediately to the south, Chemise Mountain drops off into the deep canyon of Whale Gulch, the route of the rest of this trail. The Sinkyone Wilderness and precipitous Anderson Cliffs lie just beyond. On a clear day you can spot at least 13 different coastal ridges to the south.

HIDDEN VALLEY
CHEMISE MOUNTAIN
WHALE GULCH:

DISTANCE: 7 miles one way to Whale Gulch.
  5 miles round trip to Chemise Mountain.

TIME: 3-4 hours.

TERRAIN: Through chaparral to a lush meadow, then climbing along edge of forest to ridge, which you follow to its summit. Then descend the ridge into a deep canyon to its mouth on the coast.

ELEVATION GAIN/LOSS: Hidden Valley to Chemise Mountain: 960 feet+/80 feet-
  Hidden Valley to Whale Gulch: 1170 feet+/2880 feet-

BEST TIME: Spring. Summer and fall are also good.

WARNINGS: No water on trail. Watch out for timber rattlers and poison oak. Nearest year-round facilities at Shelter Cove. South end of trail is very brushy; wear or carry long pants. Stay on trail and off private property.

DIRECTIONS TO TRAILHEAD: Leave Highway 101 at Garberville (M.11.4) on the south or at Redway (M.14.6) on the north. Take Briceland Road from Redway (2.8 miles north of Garberville on old Highway 101) for 17 miles. Go left on Chemise Mountain Road for ¼ mile to trailhead on right.

FURTHER INFO: Bureau of Land Management: (707) 822-7648 in Arcata; (707) 462-3873 in Ukiah.

OTHER SUGGESTION: A shorter, easier route to CHEMISE MOUNTAIN leaves from Wailaki Campground, 1.5 miles south of Hidden Valley Trailhead on Chemise Mountain Road. WHALE GULCH can be reached from Briceland Road in Sinkyone Wilderness State Park.

Returning to the main trail, you head south along the ridge. You meet the old Chemise-to-beach trail in 250 feet. Because of huge landslides along the coast, this trail is no longer passable to the beach. The ridge trail continues south, coming to the secondary peak of Chemise Flat at 2¾ miles.

The trail south descends briefly, then climbs to a brushy knob on the ridge at 2⅞ miles. Then you descend gently on a rocky, well-cleared path until 3⅛ miles. Your trail descends steeply, then moderately, along the west side of the ridge before it climbs to a top at 3¼ miles where bay laurel grows. You descend again with more views south.

You can hear the distant roar of surf as you climb to another top at 3¾ miles. Then a shady portion of trail descends along the ridge before climbing briefly to the top called Manzanita at 4 miles from your trailhead. A USGS bench marker beside the trail indicates an elevation of 2120 feet. This is your last good chance to turn back. From here the trail descends to sea level in less than 3 miles, becoming steep, overgrown, and occasionally hard to follow where it has not been reconstructed.

What the heck, you say? Let's go! You can reach the beach in an hour or two. Your trail descends southeast. By 4¼ miles you enter cool, mature Douglas fir forest. You leave the ridge to descend steeply into a gully by switchbacks, then contour to return to the ridge at 4⅜ miles.

The trail descends steeply along the ridge, then levels briefly at a grassy clearing, a sign of what lies ahead. You bend left and descend through mixed forest before climbing to another knob on the ridge at 4¾ miles. Your trail levels along the shady ridgetop, then descends gradually after 5 miles before leveling again. Wild rose, Douglas iris, sugar stick and huckleberry grow beneath the dense forest canopy.

Before 5½ miles you make a brief steep descent, then climb along the crest of the razor ridge, with grasslands to the west. This quickly brings you into a grassy clearing, with excellent views south into the Sinkyone Wilderness. You descend, then climb through the grasslands, then descend steeply through the forest for ⅛ mile. At 5⅞ miles you again descend through grasslands sprinkled with poppy, yarrow, redwood sorrel, tall brodiaea, buttercup, purple bush lupine, paintbrush and sticky monkeyflower. You soon meet a road from the left that the trail follows, climbing to a flattop on the ridge at 6 miles. An unfinished hip-roofed building sits beside the trail. From here you should stay on top of the ridge or on its west face; private property lies to the east.

Enjoy the easy descent through the grasslands. The trail will soon turn steep and brushy. At 6¼ miles you return to the forest as you descend steeply along the narrow ridge. As you pass the bench marker called Red Hill (elevation 1418 feet), you can see a private house below on the left. Stay on the razor ridge to avoid the private property.

Beyond the house, the trail has been brushed but not graded. Watch for poison oak from here to the bottom. At 6⅜ miles the trail veers left and follows the east side of the ridge through hardwood forest. Return briefly to the ridge. Then, at 6½ miles, the overgrown trail descends east by switchbacks, dropping through an area where Douglas firs have been cut and left lying on the ground. If you miss the brushy switchbacks you can walk the fallen logs. By 6⅝ miles the trail again becomes a broad, cleared path along or just east of the ridge. Slink pod and hazel grow on the forest floor.

At 6¾ miles your broad path passes beneath large Douglas firs. The flagged route of the planned improved trail descends east by switchbacks here, but there is no way to cross Whale Gulch Creek on that route. You should continue south along the razor ridge, descending steeply through grasslands and some brush.

At 6⅞ miles, 5 fir snags stand along the razor ridge. At the fifth snag, just beside the trail, a rough trail descends the east side of the ridge, dropping steeply to the creek. (If you do not find the trail, *be careful*—steep cliffs are hidden in the brush.) Although the path is steep and overgrown, it is safe. Rock-hop across the creek and walk downstream about 250 feet to meet the main trail.

From there a well-beaten trail climbs east by switchbacks, then levels as it passes two small lakes, 7 miles from the Hidden Valley Trailhead. The trail heads southeast, coming to Jones Beach Environmental Camp at 7⅝ miles. Three campsites are around a eucalyptus grove beside a small creek. It is one mile farther south to Needle Rock Visitor Center, where you must register if you wish to camp.

If you plan to continue on the Lost Coast Trail to Usal, you must walk the dirt road south for 2¾ miles to its end at Orchard Creek. From there it is 16¾ miles to Usal. See Trail #48.

168

SINKYONE WILDERNESS
STATE PARK

Located in the extreme northwestern corner of Mendocino County, the Sinkyone (sing-key-own) preserves a sample of the rugged wilderness that once existed all along the Humboldt Coast. Though the Sinkyone was settled in the 1860s and was logged and ranched for much of the next century, it now stands as a largely pristine wilderness. The state park was established in 1976.

The Sinkyone Wilderness State Park (7000 acres) is unlike any other park in the state system. It can be reached only by isolated, unpaved mountain roads that are often impassable in winter. You must hike at least 200 feet to camp in the northern half of the park. The Visitor Center is located in a rustic old ranch house with no electricity or telephone.

The Sinkyone was named for the Indian tribe that originally inhabited this rugged country. They were the southernmost of the Athabascan language tribes on the coast. Though known for their backwoods skills, the Sinkyone tribe was small and disorganized. They were quickly overrun by white settlers.

On the brighter side, a four-legged group of Sinkyone natives have recently been relocated in the park. At last count 24 Roosevelt elk live within park boundaries. If you meet elk on the trail, give them plenty of room, especially in rut season in September. The half-ton bulls may resent sharing their territory. When agitated, they can run as fast as 35 mph.

For more trails in Sinkyone Wilderness State Park, see the Hiker's hip pocket Guide to the Mendocino Coast.

48.

NEW LOST COAST
HEART OF THE SINKYONE

The New Lost Coast Trail traverses the most spectacular portion of the Sinkyone, a rugged, untamed country. You pass remnants of century-old homesteads and logging camps, even walk through a ghost town abandoned in 1960. But most signs of habitation have been erased by the harsh climate and lush vegetation.

This trail, completed in 1986, does not show on USGS topo maps. The California Coastal Trails Foundation publishes Trails of the Lost Coast, *the best mapping of the trail to date. On the ground, the northern third of the trail is well marked;*

the rest is generally adequate. Map and compass are recommended, as is hiking with a friend. You must register to camp along the trail. The cost is $2 per person per night.

From the road-end the trail crosses Orchard Creek on a small footbridge. The nearly level trail parallels the creek through lush, riparian vegetation. At ⅛ mile a spur on the left leads to Railroad Creek Environmental Camp. Before ½ mile you come to the site of Bear Harbor Ranch, where Bear Harbor Environmental Camp lies near the beach.

The Lost Coast Trail heads east along a creek, passing a corral and trail register. Grasslands give way to forest as you begin to climb. At ⅞ mile you cross the creek. Then you switchback to the right and climb steadily out of the canyon. Before 1¼ miles your trail joins the first of many old logging roads it follows. It climbs to grand views of the rugged coast.

At 1½ miles the trail switches away from one logging road and promptly joins another. Redwood, huckleberry, wild rose, iris, and slink pod grow along the trail. You top a ridge, then descend into Duffys Gulch. The trail leaves the logging road and joins a portion of the original Humboldt Trail, built

---

NEW LOST COAST:

DISTANCE: 16¾ miles, one way.

TIME: 3 days.

TERRAIN: Rugged coastal canyons and ridges.

ELEVATION GAIN/LOSS: To Wheeler: 1200 ft.+/1200 ft.-
Bear Harbor to Usal: 5100 feet+/5100 feet-

BEST TIME: Spring. Summer and fall are next best.

WARNINGS: Isolated country far from towns and services. Timber rattlesnakes, ticks, poison oak, stinging nettles all occur along trail; watch for them. You must have a permit to camp overnight on the trail. Camping allowed only in designated areas.

DIRECTIONS TO TRAILHEAD: Exit Highway 101 at Garberville (M.11.4) on the south or Redway (M.14.6) on the north. Take Briceland Road from Redway (2.8 miles north of Garberville on old 101). In 12 miles go left through Whitethorn. In 4.5 more miles you come to the junction known as Four Corners. Go straight, passing the Visitor Center in 3.6 miles. Then continue to trailhead at end of road.

FEES: $2/person/day.

FURTHER INFO: Sinkyone Wilderness State Park (707) 946-2311, 247-3318.

---

in 1862 when the coast to the south was opened to homesteading. Settlers from Mendocino had to ride or walk the trail to Eureka to register their land claims.

As you descend east into Duffys Gulch, you spot virgin redwoods. The trail switchbacks down to the creek crossing, passing ancient redwoods of 10 feet in diameter, grand fir, Douglas fir, bay laurel, and big leaf maple.

Take a minute to quench your thirst, fill your canteen, and marvel at the virgin beauty of this place. Along the creek grow five-finger, woodwardia, leather, sword and lady ferns. Pacific waterleaf and piggyback plant thrive in this moist habitat, as does poison oak, which you should watch for. You have come 2¼ miles from Orchard Creek.

At 2¾ miles from the trailhead, leave the forest for steep coastal grasslands. Your trail traverses the grassy bluffs through a series of small gullies and rises. Paintbrush, buttercup, blue-eyed grass, lupine, and golden poppy add color as the roar of surf rises from below.

At 2⅞ miles you plunge into the first of several dark forests along the ridge. After more grasslands, you enter another fir forest as you wrap around a sinkhole on your left. Notice the dense vegetation growing in its shelter. You pass a gnarled, wind-topped redwood, then come to more grasslands.

At 3¼ miles you come to a nice stand of redwoods. Your trail switchbacks left and climbs to the ridge. Climb steeply along the narrow ridge to its top, passing trillium, iris, redwood sorrel, one-leaved wild onion, slink pod, miners lettuce and columbine. You parallel an old fence before descending steeply east, then south. Climb steeply again to another top, then descend more switchbacks before climbing to a third top at 3¾ miles. From here you can look east into the heavily wooded canyons of Jackass Creek, site of the logging ghost town of Wheeler.

Descend gradually along the east side of the ridge through forest. Then you switch sharply right and descend bluffs of low brush and grass with foxgloves, tall broadiaeas, blue-eyed grass, sticky monkeyflowers and beach strawberries, not to mention poison oak. At 3⅞ miles you parallel the edge of a forest. At 4⅛ miles your trail leaves coast and ridge to descend southeast by a series of long switchbacks.

You soon pass two large redwoods surrounded by smaller redwoods, then descend into a fern-filled gulch. Come to big trees at the bottom of the canyon. This is known as Schoolmarm Grove, named for the Wheeler schoolhouse once located nearby. A campsite sits beneath two large redwoods in a clearing beside the North Fork of Jackass Creek. A second campsite lies 200 feet downstream, near the creek crossing. A spring is in the gulch to the west.

Wheeler was established in 1950, one of the last company logging towns and probably the newest ghost town in the west. The town lasted 10 years, abandoned as improved roads allowed the logs to be hauled to larger mills. Wheeler housed 32 families who harvested the timber, worked in the sawmill, and hauled the cut lumber to Willits by truck. The modern town had electricity, telephones and a water system.

The trail into "town" crosses the creek on a large log, remnant of an old bridge. Then the trail heads south on the old road, passing crumbling foundations, rusting logging relics and side streets. Domesticated plants grow wild here: foxglove, spearmint, red hot poker and alyssum. About ¼ mile from the creek crossing, you come to the heart of town. The sawmill was located here at the confluence of the two forks of the creek.

The trail crosses the creek and heads south, paralleling the beach at 4⅞ miles from the trailhead. A large grassy flat and a lagoon lie between the trail and the beach. High cliffs guard the dark sand beach at both ends.

The trail turns southeast and climbs a grassy gulch where the bosses lived. At 5⅛ miles you come to a wildflower garden at the top of the cleared portion of the gulch. The trail climbs steeply through dense brush, then into tall forest. At 6¾ miles you climb by several switchbacks to top a ridge at 700 feet elevation.

You descend along the border between forest and grasslands. At 7¼ miles a vernal pool lies ⅛ mile west of the trail. Continue your descent into a hanging valley of grasslands sprinkled with wildflowers. At 7½ miles you approach the creek at an elevation of 360 feet. Be careful as you cross it because stinging nettles cover deep holes in the creek; one false step and they will sting you.

Then your trail climbs east, following the south fork of the creek. At 7⅝ miles you switch right and climb a ridge at the top of Anderson Cliff by a dozen switchbacks. Several of the westernmost switchbacks have side trails that lead to the top of Anderson Cliff for magnificent views.

The long climb ends as you gain a grassy ridge at 8⅜ miles (1050 feet elevation). An old jeep road on your left climbs to meet the Wheeler Road. After a brief level stretch, your trail descends gradually east, then steeply south toward Little Jackass Creek. At 8⅞ miles you switch left and descend by several switchbacks through grasslands with great views. You can hear the herd of sea lions barking on the beach below. Wildflowers brighten the way: foxglove, paintbrush, yarrow, monkeyflower, poppy and brodiaea.

You come to the floor of the canyon at 9¼ miles, near an old corral, all that remains of a pre-1900 logging camp. An outhouse at the junction serves two adjacent campsites. The magnificent beach lies about ⅛ mile west, bordered by sea caves and the towering Anderson Cliff. A herd of sea lions lives on the south end of the beach. Please stay at least 200 feet from the wild animals.

The main trail heads up the canyon, crossing the creek at 9⅜ miles. In another 500 feet, you come to the upper camp with two more sites near the creek beneath large redwoods and maples.

The trail south starts climbing immediately, crossing the creek and ascending along it before switching right. You climb steadily by six switchbacks into the upper canyon, a checkerboard of clearcuts and virgin stands. At 10¼ miles the trail meets an old road. You follow it east, then south above Northport Gulch. The road stays generally level, crossing a small creek at 10½ miles, then passing whole hillsides of sticky monkeyflowers.

After 10⅞ miles come to a broad landing where the road turns northeast. Your trail leaves the road here, descending south, with views down to the mouth of Northport Gulch. Switch left, then descend steeply by eight switchbacks into Anderson Gulch. At 11¾ miles you reach the camp, with a view down to the mouth of Anderson Gulch.

You cross the creek after two more switchbacks. A short climb brings you to steep, grassy headlands, which you contour above the shore. Make a short descent into fern-filled Dark Gulch, which you follow upstream, crossing the creek at 12⅞ miles.

Now you make one last long ascent, climbing 900 feet in 1¼ miles to just below the 1320-foot summit of Timber Point. Your trail meanders south through the forest, crosses a seasonal creek, then descends to grasslands at 15¼ miles. An unusual red and green brodiaea called chinese firecracker grows beside the trail in spring.

You follow the ridge southeast, with great views of the coast to the south and the wooded canyons of Hotel Gulch and Usal Creek to the east. The last ⅞ mile you descend east by 20 switchbacks to meet Usal Road, 16¾ miles from the northern trailhead.

49.

PIONEER MEADOW LOOP

A DYING MEADOW AND RUSTING RELICS

Water is the focus for the 786-acre Benbow Lake State Recreation Area. The South Fork of the Eel River winds through the park, offering steelhead fishing in winter. In summer the river is dammed to form Benbow Lake, which provides swimming, fishing, canoeing (rentals available), and sailboarding. The park also has several miles of hiking trails for exploring the wooded ridges in a big bend of the river, as well as the shorelines of lake and river. You seldom see many people once you leave the trailhead.

During most of the year you must start your hike from campsite 11. Only in summer is the upper loop of the campground open, which allows you to start at campsite 73. From campsite 11, head north to parallel the chain-link fence near the freeway. As you walk through grasslands scattered with oaks and firs, you may see pretty yellow globe lilies flowering in spring. The trail passes under the freeway, coming to the upper campground. As the trail forks, you can go left along the fence to meet the Otter Trail, which follows the South Fork upstream. The described route takes the right fork west through the campground, passing the restroom at ¼ mile, then following the road for 200 feet to the real trailhead beside campsite 73.

The Pratt Mill Trail heads uphill past large redwoods, then bends right and passes through second-growth forest. At ⅜ mile you descend into a moist gully, then climb by switchbacks to a junction at ⅝ mile. Go left here. (You will return on the right fork.) In 150 feet you meet the Pioneer Trail, where you go right.

The Pioneer Trail climbs west on an old skid road. Just beyond ¾ mile, the unmarked Ridge Trail branches left. (You can add ⅞ mile and an exhilarating climb to this 2¾-mile loop by taking the Ridge Trail, which climbs to a 973-foot peak with fine views, then loops back to the Pioneer Trail.) Continuing straight on the Pioneer Trail, you wind in and out of small gullies, staying mostly level.

At 1⅛ miles the Pioneer Trail veers right, where the ridge

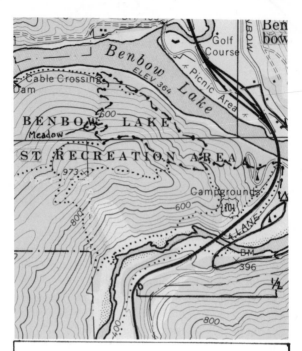

PIONEER MEADOW LOOP:

DISTANCE: 2¾- or 3⅝-mile loop (from campsite 11).

TIME: 1½ hours or more.

TERRAIN: Wooded canyons and ridges above the Benbow
Valley.

ELEVATION GAIN/LOSS: 640 feet+/640 feet-

Add+/-200 feet to ridge

BEST TIME: Spring for wildflowers, summer to jump in the
lake.

WARNINGS: Watch for poison oak.

DIRECTIONS TO TRAILHEAD: Leave Highway 101 at Benbow exit. From north at M.8.5, go left. From south at
M.8.35, go right. Then go right again for one mile. Turn
right at campground entrance, cross the river, and drive
to north end of campground. Trail leaves from campsite
11 in off season, campsite 73 in summer.

FEES: $3 day use; $10 camping.

FURTHER INFO: Benbow State Recreation Area (707)
923-3238.

loop returns to meet it. You descend gradually for 300 feet, then descend by switchbacks into virgin redwood forest. At 1⅜ miles your trail levels and comes to Pioneer Meadow. This is not so much a meadow as a grassy glade overgrown with large black oaks. Virgin redwoods and Douglas firs surround it. An uncommon place in the redwood forest, it makes a pleasant blanket-picnic spot.

The trail follows the eastern edge of the meadow. At 1½ miles you descend north by steep switchbacks. As your descent eases, you can see the inviting blue-green waters of Benbow Lake below. You soon meet the Pratt Mill Trail, which is a rutted road at this point.

Go right on Pratt Mill Trail, climbing briefly, then descending, with views of Benbow Inn across the lake. You follow the shore of the lake through a forest of large redwoods. At 1¾ miles Pratt Mill Trail leaves the road, veering right. In 100 feet you come to the site of Pratt Redwood Mill. An old boiler and drive wheels sit rusting beneath virgin redwoods. How incongruous that a redwood sawmill was shaded by these big trees!

The trail continues southeast on the old mill road and climbs a steep hill. At 2 miles you come to an overlook high above the shore of the lake, with the picnic area and Benbow Inn on the opposite bank. Then your trail veers away from the lake, climbing steadily. As your climb eases, you reach the junction with the campground loop at 2⅛ miles. Go left here, returning on the path you started out on. You come to campsite 73 at 2½ miles. It is another ¼ mile back to campsite 11.

50.

RICHARDSON GROVE STATE PARK

TANOAK SPRINGS/DURPHY CREEK LOOP

The Sinkyone Indians had a winter village on the South Fork of the Eel River near the present southern park boundary. The village of Kahs'chosoningibe had six houses constructed of slabs of redwood bark. The people of the village spent about six months of each year there, catching salmon and other fish.

The Tanoak Springs/Durphy Creek Loop is the longest hike in Richardson Grove. It explores a high ridge and a stream canyon in the southwest quadrant of the park. Other trails are listed in "Other Suggestions."

The trail heads southwest, climbing gradually through mixed forest of redwood, Douglas fir, tanoak and madrone to a fork in 150 feet. Go left on the Lookout Point Trail, heading southeast. This trail climbs gradually, following the top edge of the river canyon. Soon you switchback to the right and climb up and around a steep side canyon. You cross it at ¼ mile and climb east.

In 300 feet you come to Lookout Point, where you have a fine view of the river and highway snaking below. Then climb gradually southwest. As you pass under a power line, the trail steepens, becoming gradual again after ⅜ mile.

You soon pass back under the wires and come to a fork. (You can turn right for a short 1.3-mile loop.) Our described trail goes left, meeting the Tanoak Springs Trail in 300 feet. Go right and head northwest. The trail climbs gradually at first, then winds and climbs steeply to gain the top of the ridge at ¾ mile. Douglas irises and tiny calypso orchids grow along the trail in spring.

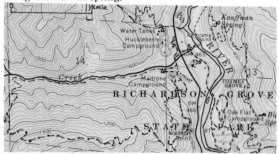

TANOAK SPRINGS/DURPHY CREEK LOOP:

DISTANCE: 4⅛-mile loop.

TIME: 2-3 hours.

TERRAIN: Up to and along a ridge, then down a creek canyon.

ELEVATION GAIN/LOSS: 950 feet+/950 feet-

BEST TIME: Spring for wildflowers. Any season is OK.

WARNINGS: Watch out for poison oak and ticks along the trail. Carry water because the spring may be dry or fouled by animals.

DIRECTIONS TO TRAILHEAD: Turn west off Highway 101 into Richardson Grove State Park at M.1.73. Go .1 mile to fork. Then go right to Madrone Campground, coming to the trailhead in another .25 mile, just past campsite 58. Restroom and water available opposite trailhead.

FEES: $3 day use. $10 camping.

FURTHER INFO: Richardson Grove State Park (707) 247-3318, 247-3378.

You climb steeply between level stretches along the ridge to 1¼ miles, where the trail runs sidehill on the steep north slope. You descend to a saddle, climb again to 1⅜ miles, then follow the level ridgetop to 1½ miles. Large madrones, tanoaks and Douglas firs grow along this part of the ridge.

Your trail stays on the ridge, climbing, descending to another saddle, then climbing into a young forest of firs at 1⅝ miles. The ridge becomes more level after this last climb.

After 1¾ miles your trail switches right and makes a winding descent to meet the side trail to Tanoak Springs at 1⅞ miles. Walk the 350 feet to the springs, where a lush patch of woodwardia ferns thrives in the cool and wet.

Returning to the main trail, turn left and descend through thickets of huckleberries. The trail makes a steep and winding descent into the canyon of Durphy Creek. At 2⅜ miles you hear the water in the creek below as big Douglas firs line the trail. You descend by about ten more switchbacks to 2¾ miles, where you head east, fifty feet above babbling Durphy Creek.

From there the trail follows the shady, north-facing south bank of the creek. The cool, moist bank shelters iris, redwood sorrel, piggyback plant, bay laurel and many ferns: sword, horsetail, chain, maidenhair and five-finger. Just before 2¾ miles, you have easy access to the creek.

Your trail descends steps to another bridge at 3⅛ miles, then quickly crosses two more bridges over side streams. Gooseberries grow here. The trail follows Durphy Creek alternating between drier and wetter microclimates. Interior live oaks with prickly leaves grow in the drier spots, while ferns, redwood sorrel and even a few western yew trees grow in the moist spots.

At 3¼ miles you draw near the creek again, but it quickly drops deeper into the canyon. You cross two more bridges at 3⅜ miles, then return to redwood forest. At 3½ miles a 12-foot-diameter redwood stands to the left of the trail.

You then descend by short switchbacks to Durphy Creek Rest at 3⅝ miles. A short side trail leads to a small redwood grove in a level spot between creek and trail, where a bench provides a picnic spot. Trilliums, redwood sorrel and calypso orchids grow beneath the big trees.

The main trail crosses two more side streams, climbs briefly, then descends through a rocky area to reach the creek bed again. From there a broad trail climbs away from the creek, coming to the paved park road in 250 feet, just before your 4-mile point.

To return to your car at the trailhead, turn right and climb the hill on the paved road to the entrance of Madrone Campground. Follow the road to campsite 58 for a total loop of 4⅛ miles.

CALIFORNIA COASTAL TRAIL

*The California Coastal Trail is a proposed 1600-mile system
of interconnected beach and coastal range trails running the
length of the spectacular California coast from Oregon to
Mexico.*

—California Coastal Trails Foundation

Although only the most avid coast hikers will hike the
California Coastal Trail (CCT) in its entirety, its establishment will provide coastal access for millions of hikers and
coast lovers. This book details access to many trails that will
become part of the CCT; this report catalogs the current
status of CCT development, from north to south.

Recent acquisitions by the California State Park System
make it possible to start at the Oregon border and walk the
coast south to Crescent City. Most recently acquired is the
area around Lakes Earl and Talawa. Environmental camps
are located north of Kellogg Road.

From Crescent City, you can follow the bike path to the
Small Boat Basin, then walk south on Crescent Beach. After
4 miles, climb to the Crescent Beach Picnic Area and walk to
the trailhead at the end of Enderts Beach Road.

The Coastal Trail runs south from there for 17 miles to
Requa (see Trails #1, 3 and 5). This portion includes several
steep climbs. Campsites along the way provide off-road
camping: Nickel Creek in the first mile and DeMartin Camp
in the ninth mile.

A hostel, opened in 1987 in a charming pioneer house,
offers accommodations at the south end of the DeMartin
Trail. It overlooks the ocean at the mouth of Wilson Creek.
The cost is $6.50 per adult per night, half price for guests
under 18 accompanied by a parent.

To continue on CCT from Requa, the Klamath River is an
obstacle, as it was to early travelers. It is 7 miles by car to the
start of the Flint Ridge Section of CCT. The distance can be
halved if someone ferries you across the Klamath.

Then the Flint Ridge Section of CCT (see Trail #6) heads
west for 4½ miles to the coast, passing Flint Ridge Camp ¼
mile from the west end. Then you can walk the Coastal Drive
for 4¼ miles to Carruthers Cove Trailhead (see Trails #7, 8).

A steep ⅞-mile descent brings you to the beach at Carruthers Cove, where 8 miles of beach walking lie to the
south. You must have a tide below +3.0 feet to walk the first
mile. After you have synchronized with the tide, it is 2¼
miles to Butler Creek Backpack Camp, but you must have
registered beforehand at the Prairie Creek Visitor Center. If
you have not pre-registered, continue south 2½ miles to the

180

Gold Bluffs Hike/Bike Camp, where you register on the spot.

From Gold Bluffs Campground, it is 1¾ miles to Espa Lagoon, starting point for the Skunk Cabbage Creek Section of CCT (see Trail #16). That trail runs 5½ miles to meet Highway 101 at the current end of this length of CCT. In the 1990s the trail will extend to Lady Bird Johnson Grove, then up the canyon of Redwood Creek.

South of Orick, you can walk the beach for 6¼ miles from Dry Lagoon to Patrick's Point (see Trail #21). A new segment of CCT from Stone Lagoon to Dry Lagoon will add 5 miles. It has been marked but will not be built before 1990.

From Little River to the mouth of Humboldt Bay lie 19 miles of beach and dunes (see Trail #28). You can walk onto the beach at Moonstone County Park, ford Little River, and walk the beach for 5 miles before you come to the mouth of Mad River. As the latter is usually too deep to ford, head east to cross the river on the Hammond Bridge, then return to the coast for another 14 miles of beach walking to the mouth of Humboldt Bay. Though you cannot cross the channel, the south spit on the other side provides another 9-mile beach to the mouth of the Eel River (see Trail #32). South of the Eel, Centerville Beach provides 9 miles of beach and dune trekking (see Trails #33 and 34). The steep cliffs between False Cape and Cape Mendocino block passage south, but south of the Cape, Mattole Road provides access to 8 miles of beach walking (see Trail #36).

The Lost Coast of the King Range may be the most famous stretch of CCT. It follows 25 miles of wilderness beach from the mouth of the Mattole River on the north to Shelter Cove on the south (see Trail #41).

From Shelter Cove, it is 3 steep miles on paved roads to the Hidden Valley Trailhead, starting point for a segment of CCT that had not been completed at press time. The Hidden Valley/Chemise Mountain/Whale Gulch Trail (see Trail #47) is steep but excellent for 4 miles. The final 3 miles to Whale Gulch had not been reconstructed in June 1988, though the author walked the steep, brushy route. A boundary dispute has delayed its completion. From Whale Gulch it is 1½ miles to the Visitor Center of Sinkyone Wilderness State Park. Then you walk 2.7 miles on unpaved Briceland Road to the New Lost Coast Trailhead, start of another 16¾-mile section of CCT (see Trail #48).

The above trails include 151 miles of coastal access, a great start for the California Coastal Trail. If you would like more information about CCT and what you can do to help, contact the Trails Coordinator, California Coastal Trails Foundation, P.O. Box 20073, Santa Barbara, CA 93120.

CROSS REFERENCE LISTING

TRAILS FOR HANDICAPPED ACCESS

12. Elk Prairie—see other suggestion
17. Lost Man Creek
18. Lady Bird Johnson Grove Loop
37. Avenue of the Giants—see M.20.5: Founders Grove

Following may be passable under best conditions or with
   assistance
24A. Elk Head
30. Arcata Marsh—first loop
31. Elk River Wildlife Refuge

TRAILS FOR BACKPACKING

1. Last Chance Section, Coastal Trail
2. DeMartin Section, Coastal Trail
6. Flint Ridge Section, Coastal Trail
7. Coastal Drive
8. Carruthers Cove—see other suggestion
11. West Ridge/Prairie Creek Loop
13. James Irvine (to Gold Bluffs Beach Hike/Bike Camp)
19. Redwood Creek
20. Tall Trees/Emerald Ridge Loop
39. Grasshopper Peak
40. Squaw Creek Ridge
41. Lost Coast—Mattole River South
42. Smith-Etter Road to Beach
43. Kings Crest North
44. Lightning Trail to Kings Peak
45. Kings Crest South
46. Shelter Cove North
47. Hidden Valley/Chemise Mountain/Whale Gulch
48. New Lost Coast

TRAILS FOR MOUNTAIN BIKES

7. Coastal Drive
9. Ossagon—see other suggestion: 17½-mile loop
10. Brown Creek—see other suggestion
28. Mad River Beach—see other suggestion: Hammond
   Trail
29. Arcata's Redwood Park—see map
39. Grasshopper Peak—see map
40. Squaw Creek Ridge—see map: 11-mile loop
42. Smith-Etter Road to Beach
43. Kings Crest North
45. Kings Crest South
47. Hidden Valley/Chemise—impassable to Whale Gulch

TRAILS FOR EQUESTRIANS

19. Redwood Creek—see other suggestion: 27 miles
24A. Elk Head—see other suggestion
28. Mad River Beach
29. Arcata's Redwood Park—see map
32. Table Bluff County Park
33. Centerville Beach North
34. Centerville Beach South
37. Avenue of the Giants—see M.8.0: Dry Creek Horse Trail
39. Grasshopper Peak—see map
40. Squaw Creek Ridge—see map
41. Mattole River South
42. Smith-Etter Road to Beach
43. Kings Crest North
44. Lightning to Kings Peak
45. Kings Crest South
46. Shelter Cove North
47. Hidden Valley/Chemise—impassable to Whale Gulch
48. New Lost Coast

BEACH WALKS (OR RUNS)

1. Enderts Beach—see also other suggestion: Crescent Beach
5. Hidden Beach
7. Coastal Drive—see Dad's Camp
15. Beach Trail (and all of Gold Bluffs Beach)
16. Skunk Cabbage Creek (north portion)
21. Dry Lagoon to Big Lagoon—see also other suggestion: Stone Lagoon
22. Agate Beach
24A. College Cove
24B. Trinidad State Beach
26. Indian Beach
27. Other Trinidad Trails
28. Mad River Beach and Dune
32. Table Bluff County Park
33. Centerville Beach North
34. Centerville Beach South
36. Cape Mendocino
41. Mattole River South—the ultimate!
46. Shelter Cove North

COMMON & SCIENTIFIC NAMES OF PLANTS ALONG THE TRAILS

* alyssum, *Lobularia maritima*

anemone (wind flower), *Anemone deltoidia*

azalea (western azalea), *Rhododendron occidentale*

baby blue eyes, *Nemophila menziesii*

bay laurel, (Calif. bay, pepperwood), *Umbellularia californica*

beach morning glory, *Calystegia soldanella*

beach pea, *Lathyrus japonicus var. glaber*

beach primrose, *Oenothera cheiranthifolia*

beach strawberry, *Fragaria chiloensis*

bear grass, *Xerophyllum tenax*

big leaf maple, *Acer macrophyllum*

Bishop pine, *Pinus muricata*

black crowberry, *Empetrum nigrum*

black oak (Calif.), *Quercus kelloggi*

black twinberry, *Lonicera involucrata*

bleeding heart (western), *Dicentra formosa*

blueblossom (Calif. lilac), *Ceanothus thyrsiflorus*

blue dick, *Brodiaea capitata*

blue-eyed grass, *Sisyrinchium bellum*

blue flag iris, *Iris purdyi*

* blue gum eucalyptus,
    Eucalyptus globulus

bracken fern, *Pteridium
    aquilinum var. pubescens*

brodiaea (tall brodiaea),
    Brodiaea laxa

brook foam, *Boykinia
    elata*

buttercup,
    Ranunculus repens

California blackberry,
    Rubus vitifolius

California poppy
    (golden poppy),
    Eschscholtzia californica

California water hemlock,
    Cicuta douglasii

* calla lily, *Zantedeschia
    aethiopica*

calypso orchid,
    Calypso bulbosa

canyon gooseberry,
    Ribes menziesii

canyon live oak,
    Quercus chrysolepis

cascara sagrada,
    Rhamnus purshiana

cattail, *Typha sp.*

chamise,
    Adenostoma fasciculatum

chicks and hens,
    Dudleya farinosa

chinese firecrackers,
    Brodiaea ida-maia

chinquapin,
    Castanopsis chrysophylla

clintonia,
    Clintonia andrewsiana

coastal manroot
    (wild cucumber),
    Marah oreganus

coast buckwheat,
    Eriogonum latifolium

coast lily, *Lilium maritimum*

coast silktassel,
    Garrya elliptica

Columbia lily,
    Lilium columbianum

columbine,
    Aquilegia formosa

coral root orchid,
    Corallorhiza sp.

* cotoneaster, *Cotoneaster sp.*

cow parsnip,
    Heracleum lanatum

coyote brush,
    Baccharis pilularis

* creeping myrtle, *Vinca minor*

cypress, *Cupressus sp.*

dandelion,
    Taraxacum officinale

deer fern, *Blechnum spicant*

dogwood (Pacific),
    Cornus nuttalli

Douglas fir,
    Pseudotsuga menziesii

Douglas iris,
    Iris douglasiana

duck weed,
    Lemna minima

elderberry (red),
    Sambucus callicarpa

evergreen huckleberry
    (Calif. huckleberry),
    Vaccinium ovatum

evergreen violet
    (redwood violet),
    Viola sempervirens

fairy lantern,
    Disporum smithii

false lily of the valley,
    Maianthemum dilatum

false solomon's seal,
    Smilacina racemosa

filaree (redstem
    storksbill),
    Erodium cicutarium

fireweed,
    Epilobium sp.

five-finger fern,
    *Adiantum pedatum
    var. aleuticum*

foxglove, *Digitalis purpurea*

giant horsetail,
    Equisetum telmateia

godetia (farewell to spring),
    Clarkia sp.

grand fir, *Abies grandis*

gum plant, *Grindelia stricta*

hairy manzanita,
    *Arctostaphylos
    columbiana*

hazel (California)
    Corylus cornuta californica

Himalayan blackberry,
    Rubus procerus

huckleberry, *Vaccinium sp.*

iceplant,
    Mesembryanthemum sp.

Indian paintbrush,
    Castilleja sp.

Indian pink,
    Silene californica

Indian warrior,
    Pedicularis densiflora

inside-out flower,
    Vancouveria dilatatum

knobcone pine,
    Pinus attenuata

lady fern,
    *Athyrium filix-femina
    var. sitchenense*

laurel,
    Umbellularia californica

leather fern
    (leather leaf fern),
    Polypodium scouleri

leopard lily,
    Lilium pardalinum

licorice fern,
    Polypodium glycyrrhiza

lupine, *Lupinus latifolius, L.
    littoralis, L. nanus,
    L. polyphyllus,
    L. variicolor, L. rivularis*

madrone, *Arbutus menziesii*

manzanita,
    Arctostaphylos sp.

miners lettuce,
    Montia sibirica

mitrewort, *Mitella ovalis*

monkeyflower,
    *Mimulus guttatus
    ssp. litoralis*

* Monterey cypress, *Cupressu.
    macrocarpa*

* Monterey pine,
    Pinus radiata

northern dune tansy,
    Tanacetum douglasii

ocean spray (cream bush)
    Holodiscus discolor

oenanthe,
    Oenanthe sarmentosa

one-leaved wild onion,
    Allium unifolium

Oregon grape,
    Mahonia nervosa

osoberry,
    Osmaronia cerasiformis

Pacific dogwood,
    Cornus nuttallii

Pacific waterleaf,
    Hydrophyllum tenuipes

paintbrush,
    *Castilleja latifolia,
    C. affinis, C. foliolosa,
    C. hololeuca, C. wightii,
    C. mendosensis*

* pampas grass,
    Cortaderia selloana

pennyroyal (western),
    Monardella lanceolata

piggyback plant,
    Tolmiea menziesii

plantain, *Plantago sp.*

* poison hemlock,
    Conium maculatum

poison oak,
    Toxicodendron diversiloba

poppy,
    Eschscholzia californica

Port Orford cedar,
    *Chamaecyparis
    lawsoniana*

raspberry,
    Rubus leucodermis

red alder, *Alnus rubra*

red-flowering currant,
    Ribes sanguineum

* red hot poker,
    Kniphofia uvaria

red huckleberry, *Vaccinium
    parvifolium*

red trillium,
    Trillium choloropetalum

redwood,
    Sequoia sempervirens

redwood lily,
    Lilium rubescens

redwood sorrel,
    Oxalis oregana

rein orchid,
    *Habenaria elegans
    var. maritima*

rhododendron,
    Rhododendron macrophyllum

rush, *Juncus sphaerocarpus*

salal, *Gaultheria shallon*

salmonberry,
    Rubus spectabilis

sand verbena, yellow,
    Abronia latifolia

sand verbena, pink,
    Abronia maritima

* Scotch broom,
    Cytisus scoparius

scouring rush,
    Equisetum hyemale

sea fig (iceplant),
  Mesembryanthemum chilense

sea rocket,
  Cakile maritima

seaside daisy,
  Erigeron glaucus

sea thrift, *Armeria maritima
  var. californica*

sedge, *Carex sp.*

shore pine, *Pinus contorta
  ssp. contorta*

silky beach pea,
  Lathyrus littoralis

silverweed, *Potentilla egedei
  var. grandis*

Sitka spruce,
  Picea sitchensis

skunk cabbage,
  Lysichitum americanum

slink pod,
  scoliopus bigelovii

* spearmint, *Mentha spicata*

starflower,
  Trientalis latifolia

star solomon's seal,
  Smilacina stellata

sticky monkeyflower,
  Mimulus aurantiacus

stinging nettle, *Urtica lyalli*

sugar pine,
  Pinus lambertiana

sugarstick,
  Allotropa virgata

sundew,
  Drosera rotundifolia

sword fern,
  Polystichum munitum

tanoak,
  Lithocarpus densiflorus

tansy (dune tansy),
  Tanacetum douglasii

thimbleberry, *Rubus parviflorus*

thistle, *Cirsium brevistylum*

tooth-leaved monkeyflower,
  Mimulus dentalus

trillium, *Trillium chloropetalum,
  T. ovatum*

twisted stalk,
  Streptopus amplexifolius

vanilla leaf (deer foot),
  Achlys triphylla

vetch, *Vicia angustifolia*

vine maple, *Acer circinatum*

watercress,
  Nasturtium officiriale

wax myrtle (bayberry),
  Myrica californica

western coltsfoot,
  Petasites palmatus

western hemlock,
  Tsuga heterophylla

western yew,
  Taxus brevifolia

whitethorn,
  Ceanothus incanus

wild ginger,
  Asarum caudatum

wild mustard,
  Brassica campestris

wild rose, *Rosa sp.*

wild tobacco,
  Nicotiana attenuata

willow, *Salix sp.*

wintergreen, *Pyrola sp.*

wood fern, *Dryopteris arguta*

woodwardia fern,
  Woodwardia fimbriata

yarrow, *Achillea borealis
  ssp. californica*

yellow globe lily (fairy
  lantern),
  Calochortus amabilis

yellow pond lily,
  Naphar polysepalum

yerba de selva,
  whipplea modesta

* Introduced species

BIBLIOGRAPHY

Adams, Kramer, *The Redwoods*, Popular Library, New York, 1968.

Alt, David D. and Donald W. Hyndman, *Roadside Geology of Northern California*, Mountain Press Publishing Co., Missoula, Montana, 1975.

Becking, Rudolph. *Pocket Flora of the Redwood Forest.* Island Press, Covelo, Ca., 1982.

Brown, Joseph E., *Monarchs of the Mist*, Coastal Parks Assoc., Pt. Reyes, Ca., 1982.

California Coastal Access Guide, University of California Press, Berkeley, 1983.

California Coastal Resource Guide, University of California Press, Berkeley, 1987.

Chase, J. Smeaton, *California Coastal Trails*, Tioga Publishing, Palo Alto, Ca., 1987, reprint, originally published: Houghton Mifflin, Boston, 1913.

Chronic, Halke, *Pages of Stone: Geology of Western National Parks and Monuments: Sierra Nevada, Cascades and Pacific Coast, Volume 2,* Mountaineers, Seattle, Wa., 1986.

Coy, Owen C., *The Humboldt Bay Region 1850-1875,* Calif. State Historical Association, Los Angeles, 1929.

Dawson, Ron, *Nature Bound Pocket Field Guide*, Omnigraphics Ltd., Boise, Id., 1985.

Dewitt, John B. *California Redwood Parks and Preserves,* Save-the-Redwoods League, San Francisco, 1982.

Grillos, Steve J., *Ferns and Fern Allies of California,* University of California Press, Berkeley, 1966.

Handbook of North American Indians, edited by William C. Sturtevant, Smithsonian Institution, Washington, D.C., 1978.

Hayden, Mike, *Exploring the North Coast*, Chronicle Books, San Francisco, 1982.

Hoopes, Chad L., *Lure of the Humboldt Bay Region*, Wm. C. Brown Co., Dubuque, Iowa, 1966.

Keator, Glenn and Ruth Heady, *Pacific Coast Berry Finder*, Nature Study Guild, Berkeley, 1978.

Keator, Glenn and Ruth Heady, *Pacific Coast Fern Finder*, Nature Study Guild, Berkeley, 1981.

Kroeber, A.L., *Handbook of the Indians of California*, Dover Publications, New York, 1976.

Lewis, Oscar, *The Quest for Qual-a-wa-loo (Humboldt Bay),* San Francisco, 1943, (no publisher cited).

Leydet, Francois, *The Last Redwoods and the Parklands of Redwood Creek*, Sierra Club, Ballantine Books, New York, 1969.

Little, Elbert, *The Audubon Society Field Guide to North American Trees*, Western Region, Alfred A. Knopf, New York, 1980.

McConnaughey, Bayard H. and Evelyn McConnaughey, *Pacific Coast*, Audubon Society Nature Guides, Alfred A. Knopf, New York, 1985.

Munz, Philip A., *California Spring Wildflowers*, University of California Press, Berkeley, 1961.

Munz, Philip A., *Shore Wildflowers of California, Oregon and Washington*, University of California Press, Berkeley, 1973.

Niehaus, Theodore F. and Charles L. Ripper, *Field Guide to Pacific States Wildflowers*, (Peterson Field Guide Series) Houghton Mifflin, Boston, 1976.

O'Neill-Knight, Dusty, *Humboldt Redwoods Trail Guide*, Revised, Humboldt Redwoods Interpretive Association, Weott, Ca., 1988.

Peterson, Roger Tory, *A Field Guide to Western Birds*, Houghton Mifflin, Boston, 1961.

Randall, Warren R., Robert F. Keniston and Dale N. Bever, *Manual of Oregon Trees and Shrubs*, Oregon State University Bookstores, Corvallis, Or., 1978.

Ransom, Jay Ellis, *Complete Field Guide to North American Wildlife*, Harper & Row, New York, 1981.

Russo, Ron and Pam Olhausen, *Pacific Intertidal Life*, Nature Study Guild, Berkeley, 1981.

Schrepfer, Susan R., *The Fight to Save the Redwoods*, Univ. of Wisconsin Press, Madison, 1983.

Spellenberg, Richard, *The Audubon Society Field Guide to North American Wildflowers*, Western Region, Alfred A. Knopf, New York, 1979.

Watts, Phoebe, *Redwood Region Flower Finder*, Nature Study Guild, Berkeley, 1979.

Watts, Tom, *Pacific Coast Tree Finder*, Nature Study Guild, Berkeley, 1973.

Whitney, Stephen, *Western Forests*, Audubon Society Nature Guides, Alfred A. Knopf, New York, 1985.

Yocum, Charles and Raymond Dasmann, *The Pacific Coastal Wildlife Region*, American Wildlife Region Series, Naturegraph, Happy Camp, Ca., 1965.

Young, Dorothy King, *Redwood Empire Wildflowers*, Third Edition, Naturegraph Publishers, Happy Camp, Ca., 1976.

INDEX

ABOUT BORED FEET

We established Bored Feet Publications in 1986 to publish and distribute the *Hiker's hip pocket Guides* to California's North Coast. In November, 1986, we published *The Hiker's hip pocket Guide to the Mendocino Coast.* Now in its second printing, 5000 copies have been sold in its first 19 months. This *Humboldt* book is our second publication. In 1989, we will write, produce and publish *The Hiker's hip pocket Guide to the Sonoma Coast.*

We want you to be fully informed about the trails of the North Coast. If you would like to receive updates on the trails included in our publications, send us your name and address, specifying your counties of interest.

We also operate a retail mail order business specializing in books and maps about the North Coast. If you are on our mailing list, you will receive our periodic catalogs. Your purchases directly from Bored Feet support our independent publishing efforts to bring you more information about the spectacularly scenic North Coast of California.

Thanks for your support!

Bob Lorentzen
Author/Publisher

Write: Bored Feet
        P.O. Box 1832
        Mendocino, CA 95460
Phone: (707) 964-6629